FREE
EXPRESSION
UNDER FIRE

FREE EXPRESSION UNDER FIRE

DEFENDING Free Speech and Free Press Across the POLITICAL SPECTRUM

STUART N. BROTMAN

Skyhorse Publishing

Skyhorse Publishing books may be purchased in bulk at special discounts for sales promotion, corporate gifts, fund-raising, or educational purposes. Special editions can also be created to specifications. For details, contact the Special Sales Department, Skyhorse Publishing, 307 West 36th Street, 11th Floor, New York, NY 10018 or info@skyhorsepublishing.com.

Skyhorse® and Skyhorse Publishing® are registered trademarks of Skyhorse Publishing, Inc.®, a Delaware corporation.

Visit our website at www.skyhorsepublishing.com.

10 9 8 7 6 5 4 3 2 1

Library of Congress Cataloging-in-Publication Data is available on file.

Cover design by David Ter-Avanesyan

ISBN: 978-1-5107-8675-2
Ebook ISBN: 978-1-5107-8676-9

Printed in the United States of America

For Ruby
Express Yourself Freely—Always

TABLE OF CONTENTS

Foreword by Greg Lukianoff   xiii
Introduction: Why This Matters for All of Us   xvii

PART I: THE RAPIDLY CHANGING LANDSCAPE   1

Chapter 1: Free Expression Threats in Real Time   3
Chapter 2: Beyond Cancel Culture   5
Chapter 3: Facts and Opinions Both Matter   7

PART II: CAMPUS TENSIONS   11

Chapter 4: Can Universities Coexist with Free Speech?   13
Chapter 5: Campuses Should Offer Teach-Ins on Freedom
    of Speech   19
Chapter 6: Threats on Campuses Need to Be Dealt with Directly   22
Chapter 7: Stanford Law's Free Speech Teachable Moments   25
Chapter 8: Explicitly Addressing College Self-Censorship
    in the New Academic Year   29
Chapter 9: Exploring Campus "Zero Tolerance" to Combat
    Antisemitism   32

PART III: DIGITAL TRANSFORMATION   35

Chapter 10: Why the Internet Stays Free   37
Chapter 11: First Amendment Rights Hit Turbulence in
    Cyberspace   41
Chapter 12: The TikTok Saga—National Security vs.
    Free Expression   46

Chapter 13: Elon Musk's Digital Town Square Model for
Twitter (Now X) Remains Elusive 51

Chapter 14: Creating an Internet Fairness Doctrine
Would Backfire 53

PART IV: JOURNALISM'S FREE PRESS CHALLENGES 57

Chapter 15: The Risky Game of Crowdsourced Journalism 59

Chapter 16: The Challenge of Treating Social Media Influencers
as Journalists 61

Chapter 17: Let C-SPAN Have Unrestricted Camera Access
to US House Proceedings 63

PART V: LESSONS FROM THE PAST 67

Chapter 18: *George Carlin's American Dream* Celebrates
the First Amendment 69

Chapter 19: Inside the Pentagon Papers Case—a First
Amendment Victory Story 74

Chapter 20: Let's Not Create a Self-Censorship Wave in Comedy 85

PART VI: BROADCASTING AND THE CONSTITUTION 87

Chapter 21: Airwaves Regulation and the First Amendment 89

Chapter 22: Revisiting the Broadcast Public Interest Standard
in Communications Law and Regulation 94

Chapter 23: Will the FCC's "Public Interest" Standard Limit
Broadcast Free Speech? 106

Chapter 24: A Diminishing Electronic Media Future
for Political Advertising 110

PART VII: PRACTICAL STEPS TO SUPPORT FREE EXPRESSION 113

Chapter 25: Free Speech, Free Press, Play Ball! 115

Chapter 26: The First Amendment Should Be the Next
  Movie Blockbuster   117
Chapter 27: Media Literacy for Democracy's Next Generation   119
Chapter 28: Guardrails for Fake News, Misinformation, and
  Disinformation   122
Chapter 29: The Two Questions That Can Save Us
  from Digital Deception   125
Chapter 30: America Needs a National News Council
  Once Again   128

PART VIII: GLOBAL PERSPECTIVES   137

Chapter 31: Technologies of Freedom, Revisited   139
Chapter 32: Sending a Strong Signal on Global Internet Freedom 142
Chapter 33: Ukraine War's Powerful First Amendment Lesson 146

PART IX: THE PATH FORWARD   149

Chapter 34: The Enduring Wisdom of US Supreme Court
  Justices Brandeis and Holmes   151
Chapter 35: When Senseless Violence Can Strengthen Free
  Expression Resolve   154
Chapter 36: Honoring James Madison's First Amendment
  Legacy in Today's Polarized America   157

Afterword   165
Acknowledgments   167
About the Author   171
Endnotes   173

by Greg Lukianoff

———

"Shut it down." That's what angry students shouted when a pro-Israel speaker came to UC Berkeley in 2024. Pro-Palestinian students didn't want the speech to happen, so they organized online opposition. Nearly two hundred students showed up to stop it. They attacked the event space—breaking a door, smashing a window, and eventually forcing the speaker to leave.

I have defended thousands of students' rights to free speech and protest. But no one has the right to silence someone else or decide what others can hear. Stopping a talk through force is not freedom of speech—it's mob censorship. Sadly, 2023 and 2024 were the worst years yet for protests that turned into "shout-downs" or canceled events.

Not all speech is protected, of course. Violent threats and harassment cross legal lines. If there is a true "free speech absolutist," I've never met one. I am, however, an "opinion absolutist"—I believe that all viewpoints should be open to discussion because basic free speech is a human right.

Every person's opinion offers something valuable for understanding the world, even when we disagree. That might sound counterintuitive, but I went to law school precisely because I wanted to study freedom of speech and the First Amendment.

Four Essential Truths About Free Speech

First, free speech keeps us safer. Second, free speech helps prevent violence. Third, free speech protects people with less power. Fourth, even people we disagree with can have valuable ideas.

Let me explain each truth:

1. Free Speech Makes Us Safer
My mentor, civil rights lawyer Harvey Silverglate, spent his life defending speech rights. He once said, "I'd rather know who the Nazis are in the room, so I know who not to trust." He's right. It's safer to know what people truly think than to keep dangerous ideas hidden.

2. Free Speech Helps Prevent Violence
About half of Americans now believe words can constitute violence—especially on college campuses. I've heard students shout, "Your words are violence!" at speakers they dislike.

But I've experienced real violence. I've been punched and suffered a concussion. I once watched a friend get stabbed. Confusing harsh words with actual physical violence disrespects people who have truly been hurt. Free speech is actually the best alternative to violence that society has invented.

3. Free Speech Protects the Powerless
Some people today view free speech as a tool for bullies or the wealthy. That's simply wrong. Rich and powerful people rarely need extra protection to be heard.

Freedom of speech has always mattered most to people challenging those in power or fighting for better rights. Leaders like Frederick Douglass, Ida B. Wells, Mahatma Gandhi, Martin Luther King Jr., and Nelson Mandela all championed free speech as essential for social progress. As civil rights icon John Lewis said, "Without freedom of speech, the civil rights movement would have been a bird without wings."

4. Even Flawed People Can Have Good Ideas
Too often on social media, we dismiss people's ideas simply because we dislike them personally. But history shows this is a mistake. Even people with terrible beliefs have made important discoveries. Rocket scientist Wernher von Braun, despite his Nazi past, helped land humans on the moon. Thomas Malthus developed ideas that were later misused, though he was considered a decent man. Thomas More was a saint who also burned people for their beliefs.

Someone's flawed character or reputation doesn't automatically invalidate their ideas. We learn and discover truth best through honest debate—even with people we don't like or agree with.

The Spirit of Socrates

Socrates, the great Greek philosopher, challenged people to think for themselves. He asked hard questions and upset so many Athenians that they eventually executed him. Socrates understood that absolute certainty is dangerous for our minds.

Young people—students—have often been champions of free speech, and they can be again. But success requires remembering that finding truth means truly understanding what others think. That only happens when people feel safe expressing their authentic views. For that, we must actively protect free speech for everyone.

The same spirit of questioning and open dialogue that Stuart N. Brotman champions in this book is what our democracy desperately needs today.

—Greg Lukianoff, President and CEO of the Foundation
for Individual Rights and Expression (FIRE) and
co-author of *The Coddling of the American Mind.*

INTRODUCTION

Why This Matters for All of Us

"If you had to pick one freedom that is the most essential to the functioning of a democracy, it must be freedom of speech—because democracy means persuading one another and then ultimately voting. . . . You can't run such a system if there is a muzzling of one point of view."

                    —US Supreme Court Justice Antonin Scalia

"It's hard to keep the freedom of the press because there are many people who don't like what the press is publishing. . . . So the right to speak against government—against what is the prevailing view of society—is tremendously important."

                    —US Supreme Court Justice Ruth Bader Ginsburg

Today, from college campuses to corporate boardrooms, from social media platforms to Supreme Court chambers, the fundamental freedoms that define American democracy face challenges from all sides. These aren't theoretical concerns. In the past year alone, we've seen university presidents resign over campus speech controversies, social media platforms ban major political figures, and journalists face unprecedented legal challenges.

Whether you're a student worried about speaking up in class, a parent concerned about what your children can read, a journalist facing online harassment, or a citizen trying to separate fact from fiction online, these aren't abstract constitutional questions—they're daily realities affecting your life.

My Journey to Understanding Free Expression

As someone who has participated in First Amendment cases, advised government officials, and taught constitutional law over several decades, I've seen these principles tested in courtrooms, classrooms, and newsrooms around the world. In recent years, my writing on free speech and press freedom has reached more than five hundred million readers worldwide—from students and teachers to journalists and judges, from concerned parents to engaged citizens.

But my path to understanding these issues wasn't traditional. The lessons that would shape much of my life's professional work came from an unexpected place: a suburban New Jersey high school newsroom, where I first discovered that the right to speak and report freely isn't guaranteed—it has to be fought for, every single day.

When I was a student journalist, at the height of the Vietnam anti-war movement, administrators would apply subtle pressure by suggesting, "Why don't you cover this instead?" There wasn't outright censorship—no administrator said, "You cannot publish this." But I learned from two exceptional faculty advisors, Arza Dean and Elaine Levine, that protecting both free speech and press freedom requires constant vigilance.

This was a time when we were all beginning to challenge authority. The country was changing dramatically. I remember one of our big rebellions—which sounds quaint today—was about dress codes. We staged a one-day protest where all students wore shorts. That was considered dramatic rebellion then. But it taught me that questioning authority requires having the freedom to question authority.

I continued working in media throughout college at Northwestern University, graduate school at the University of Wisconsin-Madison, and then law school at UC Berkeley, just after the historic Free Speech Movement there. That environment, where people embraced emerging values of free speech and open expression, shaped my thinking for decades to come.

From Academic Towers to Kitchen Tables

Over I began to devote my professional life to promoting and preserving freedom of expression. In the early years, I followed a traditional academic path, writing scholarly articles aimed primarily at other academics. But I realized that wasn't enough.

The world had changed dramatically. I began recognizing the importance of directing my thoughts about free speech and press freedom to much larger audiences. This led me to public scholarship—taking complex ideas out of academic ivory towers and putting them where they belong: in kitchen table conversations, coffee shop debates, and civic discussions that shape our communities.

Public scholarship means making academic knowledge accessible to everyone, not just other scholars. It means recognizing that in a democracy, everyone needs to understand their rights and responsibilities.

Why a Curated Collection?

This book represents a unique approach to understanding free expression in our time. Rather than writing a traditional academic treatise after the fact, I've curated thirty-six pieces written in real time as these challenges emerged over more than a decade—what I call "first impressions" of evolving threats to democratic discourse and reporting.

These pieces span from 2014 to 2025, covering early concerns about global internet freedom through the most recent campus speech controversies and government oversight debates. This decade-plus timeframe captures multiple presidential administrations, major technological shifts, and significant cultural changes—from the rise of TikTok to Elon Musk's Twitter acquisition and name change to X, from campus speech codes to cancel culture debates, from COVID-era restrictions to post-pandemic reassessments of authority.

Why this curatorial approach? Because free expression issues don't unfold in the neat chronological chapters that retrospective analysis might suggest. They emerge suddenly—a campus speaker is shouted down, a platform bans a political figure, a government agency investigates a news broadcast—and require immediate analysis that captures both the specific moment and the larger constitutional principles and cultural impacts at stake.

Each piece in this collection was written for a different audience at a different moment: some for legal scholars grappling with Supreme

Court precedents, others for parents worried about their children's education, still others for citizens trying to understand why their social media posts might be restricted. But taken together, they tell a larger story about how free expression challenges have evolved and what they mean for democracy's future.

I've organized these pieces not chronologically, but thematically—moving from understanding current challenges to learning from past victories to taking practical action. This structure allows you to see connections across seemingly disparate events: how a 1970s recorded comedy routine shaped today's broadcasting regulations, how campus speech codes relate to social media content policies, how historical press freedom battles inform current journalism challenges.

A Book for Multiple Audiences, a Single Democratic Purpose

This collection serves readers across the spectrum: professors can assign individual essays that illuminate specific constitutional principles; general readers can follow the complete arc from problem identification to practical solutions; practitioners can find real-world applications of abstract legal concepts.

But regardless of how you approach this book, the purpose remains the same: empowering citizens to become more informed participants in the democratic discourse that free expression makes possible.

We Don't Need Government to Lead This Change

As National Constitution Center President Jeffrey Rosen noted, "The First Amendment says Congress shall make no law. It does not say Facebook shall make no law. Facebook and Google . . . have more power over free speech than any king or president or Supreme Court Justice."

We face a fundamental cultural challenge: society needs to make decisions about how we want to deal with the First Amendment. The First Amendment is a legal construct enforced by courts, but free speech and press freedom are cultural values that extend well beyond constitutional law.

Much of what people call "wokeness" or "cancel culture" are not First Amendment issues—they're broader cultural questions about free expression. The truth is, we really don't have a robust free expression culture in this country. How do we make people more sensitive to these issues and more respectful of the First Amendment?

Cultural changes don't require government action. We can do it ourselves. Just as there was a fifty-year campaign to promote Second Amendment rights that reshaped American values, we need the same dedicated effort for the First Amendment.

Attacks on the First Amendment come from both left and right. Both sides want censorship in different ways. But both fundamentally lack a cultural understanding of free speech and press freedom as bedrock American values.

Real cultural change takes time—sometimes a generation or more. I'm not suggesting we'll see results immediately. But it's important to start now and begin developing practical steps in that direction.

What You'll Learn

In these pages, you'll discover why campus speech codes often backfire, how social media companies make decisions about your posts, what happens when governments try to regulate the internet, why press freedom faces unprecedented challenges, and most importantly, what these developments mean for democracy itself.

The complexity of emerging restrictions on both free speech and press freedom, combined with rapid technological developments, makes understanding these issues challenging. Each essay captures my thinking at the time it was written, rather than conveying rigid conclusions about free expression concerns. Together, they provide a framework for understanding not just what's happening, but why it matters and what you can do about it.

This book offers an opportunity to reflect on what free speech and press freedom mean in contemporary life—not just in the United States, but around the world. In an era when democracy itself feels fragile, understanding and defending both individual expression and journalistic freedom isn't just an academic exercise—it's a survival skill.

Your Role in Protecting Freedom

As America celebrates its 250th anniversary and looks toward its third century, this collection gives you the tools to understand free expression challenges and the complex forces that threaten both individual voices and institutional journalism. Our children's future—and our democracy's survival—depends on citizens who understand not just their rights to speak and publish, but the cultural shifts necessary to preserve these freedoms for future generations.

The time for abstract constitutional debates has passed. We need a clear, sophisticated understanding of how both free speech and press freedom function in a democratic society—and a practical wisdom to defend free expression in our daily lives.

PART I

THE RAPIDLY CHANGING LANDSCAPE

"The First Amendment of our Constitution is the most human amendment."
—Turning Point USA CEO Emma Kirk

How Free Expression Is Evolving and Why It Matters

Free expression in America has never been static, but today's challenges feel fundamentally different from those faced by previous generations. Traditional boundaries between acceptable and unacceptable expression have blurred in our digital age. Historical approaches to limiting communication may no longer serve democratic discourse, how citizens can navigate increasingly complex questions about facts and opinions, and the nature of truth itself.

CHAPTER 1

Free Expression Threats in Real Time (2025)

———

"Using the government to punish critical speech is wrong, regardless of who is in power and regardless of whether the criticism is right or fair."
—Jonah Goldberg, Senior Fellow and Asness Chair in Applied Liberty, American Enterprise Institute

Can we still speak and report openly? This critical question isn't rhetorical; it demands an honest answer. And increasingly, that answer isn't as clear as it used to be.

From newsrooms to classrooms, from corporate boardrooms to kitchen table conversations, Americans are grappling with unprecedented challenges to free expression. The twin pillars of democracy—free speech and free press—face pressure from all directions: government officials seeking to control narratives, tech platforms making content decisions, activists demanding accountability, and citizens caught in the crossfire.

The New Reality of Restricted Expression

Consider what's happened just in recent years: university presidents have resigned over campus speech controversies. Major social media platforms have banned sitting political figures. Journalists face lawsuits, death threats, and government investigations at record levels. Comedy shows self-censor to avoid controversy. Students report being afraid to speak up in class discussions.

3

This isn't the America the founders envisioned when they crafted the First Amendment's forty-five words. But it's the America we inhabit today—one where the right to speak and report freely requires constant defense.

However, as the Freedom Forum noted in its 2025 report, *Where America Stands*, "Americans are increasingly divided—not on whether the First Amendment matters, but on what it means, who it protects and how far its guarantees should go."[1]

Defining Democracy's Future

The digital age has fundamentally changed how we communicate, consume information, and engage with each other. Social media platforms have more power over expression than any government in history. Traditional journalism struggles with new economic models while facing attacks on its credibility. Academic institutions wrestle with balancing free inquiry against calls for trigger warnings and safer spaces.

These aren't just policy debates—they're questions that affect your daily life. Can you share your honest opinion at work? Should your children's school library carry certain books? How do you know what news sources to trust? When does criticism become harassment?

The Stakes Have Never Been Higher

Free speech and press freedom aren't mere constitutional niceties—they're the operating systems of democracy. When they break down, everything else follows. Authoritarian leaders always begin by attacking the press and silencing dissent. Democratic societies thrive when citizens can speak openly, and journalists can report without fear.

But protecting these freedoms isn't just the government's job. It's everyone's responsibility. And that means understanding not just what these rights protect, but how they work in practice—and what happens when they don't.

The challenge isn't merely defending expression from government censorship anymore. It's rebuilding a culture that values vigorous debate and reporting, tolerates offense, and understands that democracy depends on citizens willing to engage with ideas they find uncomfortable or wrong.

CHAPTER 2

Beyond Cancel Culture (2022)

The term "cancel culture" has become unusually pervasive in recent years. It's even reached the Vatican Diplomatic Corps, which includes representatives from the 183 countries accredited to the Holy See. There, the late Pope Francis said, "Cancel culture is invading many circles and public institutions. As a result, agendas are increasingly dictated by a mindset that rejects the natural foundations of humanity and the cultural roots that constitute the identity of many people."[1]

What Cancel Culture Really Represents

Today, cancel culture has largely been reduced to a label affixed to any call for someone or something to be publicly admonished, typically through social media and its aftermath. It is used by those along all poles of the political spectrum to point out the intolerance of the other side, sometimes even by the government itself.

But cancel culture is just a symptom of a larger social disease that has been with us since Victorian times, then amped up in the United States as it became incorporated into our American value system. Put simply, the root of cancel culture is an individual's or group's need to censor.

The Long History of American "Cancellation"

The recent blockbuster movie *Elvis* reminds us that cancel culture has been a feature of American life for decades. Many still remember how Elvis Presley's records were banned from radio stations based on his on-stage gyrations. Ed Sullivan, too, famously canceled any below-the-waist view of Elvis on his popular Sunday night TV show. A national crisis among screaming teenage girls who were not exposed to Elvis' swinging hips was thus averted, albeit temporarily.

The arrival of the Beatles didn't change things much either. When John Lennon sarcastically commented at a news conference that his group was more popular than Jesus, radio stations across the country promptly removed their music and advised that Beatles records be destroyed immediately.

The Disco Demolition Warning

Remember disco music, which became the soundtrack of our lives in the 1970s? All that was needed by the cancel culture warriors of the day was the support of radio shock jock and anti-disco campaigner Steve Dahl, along with Major League Baseball, which organized a highly publicized promotion at Chicago's Comiskey Park in 1979. There, between a Chicago White Sox–Detroit Tigers doubleheader, a crate filled with disco records was blown up by Dahl on the field. The crowd went wild—an actual riot followed among thousands in attendance, shouting the new cancel culture mantra, "Disco Sucks."

The Deeper Cultural Problem We Must Address

Similar stories are plentiful in many other areas of popular culture—comic books, movies, TV shows, and stand-up comedy. And this is not a new phenomenon for any of these, either. Everything old seems new again.

Our current focus on "cancel culture" incorrectly emphasizes *cancel* instead of *culture*. Unless and until we come to grips with why some in our society want to impose censorship on others, the cycle is sure to repeat itself many times again, to our collective detriment.

The desire to silence opposing voices runs deeper than any political moment or social movement. It reflects a fundamental misunderstanding of how democracy works—the false belief that preventing others from speaking somehow makes our own voices stronger. The opposite is true: a society that tolerates only approved speech inevitably becomes a society where fewer voices are permitted to speak at all.

CHAPTER 3

Facts and Opinions Both Matter (2022)

"Everyone is entitled to their own opinions, but not their own facts." This frequently cited quote is usually attributed to the late US Senator Daniel Patrick Moynihan and often used by those who want to end a conversation rather than continue with one.

Yet digging a bit deeper, Moynihan's certainty may be less than meets the eye. He used it as a sharp comeback during an argument he was having with a colleague, not as a reflection of wisdom. It had the intended effect of shutting down the discussion cold.

And the line most likely was not even originated on the spot, either.

The Quote's Uncertain Origins

According to word historian Barry Popik, former Defense Secretary James R. Schlesinger had included this line in his 1973 Congressional testimony, several years before it was credited to Pat Moynihan.[1]

Decades before, Bernard M. Baruch, then serving on the United Nations Atomic Energy Commission, expressed a similar sentiment more precisely: "Every man has a right to his own opinion, but no man has a right to be wrong in his facts."[2]

So ironically, even in this instance, there is an uncertain factual basis for whether the quote should be so widely attributed to Senator Moynihan at all.

The Complex Reality of Political Facts

As a practical matter, particularly in the worlds of policy and politics, there is a limited set of facts that is undisputed. Many are within the realms of history or geography. There can be no disagreement that the United States was bombed by Japan at Pearl Harbor on December 7, 1941, or that Texas borders neighboring Mexico.

But these types of facts are not the typical ones that politicians and policymakers are debating. Instead, there frequently are competing sets of facts that can change minds depending upon how they are generated or interpreted.

Budget and tax policies, for example, often are based on economic forecasts that may vary substantially based on the assumptions of individual forecasters. Their opinions thus reflect individual facts rather than ones that are agreed upon at the outset.

Why Disagreement Can Be Productive

A quick review of factual differences by the nonpartisan Congressional Budget Office and the staffs of Congressional committees illustrates that disagreements about economic facts are to be expected and may even produce better policy outcomes, since there can then be a healthy back-and-forth regarding how the respective forecasts were made.

Agreeing to disagree on the facts also may be beneficial, since there may be other forces at play, such as public sentiment, which may not be baked into a particular factual analysis.

Finding Common Ground in Democratic Discourse

There seems to be a widespread and long-standing consensus, predating Donald Trump's election in 2016, that both Democrats and Republicans agree that they do not believe the other side is expressing basic (i.e., undisputed) facts on policy.

Pew Research Center survey data from 2018 indicates overwhelming majorities from both parties are like-minded here.[3] Perhaps this is because they, too, recognize that basic facts are not the engine that drives policy development. The political context of policymaking instead suggests that everyone can be entitled to their own opinions and often their own facts.

Although this dynamic can lead to stalemates, it can also lead to searches for compromises that are not based on someone being factually wrong. This should be a ray of hope for those who think the political system is irretrievably broken due to extreme partisanship.

Facts, Opinions, and Democracy

Opinions and facts are the yin and yang of expressive activity, rather than just a linear progression of what we think makes sense. After all, most factual assumptions other than death are not 100 percent accurate forever.

By moving the Moynihan quote out of the spotlight, we can be more open to letting others know what we are thinking and why. And we may even find that we agree with what someone else is saying, even though we may be relying on our own facts to reach that conclusion.

The deeper lesson here is that democracy depends not on everyone agreeing about facts, but on everyone agreeing that debate itself has value. When we use "facts" as weapons to silence opposing viewpoints, we undermine the very process that allows democratic societies to work through complex problems over time.

PART II
CAMPUS TENSIONS

"The academy might be the last, best place where American citizens can learn to coexist, converse, and cooperate with people whose views are different than their own."
—Vanderbilt University Chancellor Daniel Diermeier

From university lecture halls to social media platforms to newsrooms, the most visible free expression conflicts of our time are reshaping how Americans think about constitutional protections. Specific institutional pressures and technological changes have made campus discourse into a testing ground for broader questions about who gets to speak, what they can say, and under what circumstances expression might be limited.

CHAPTER 4

Can Universities Coexist with Free Speech? (2025)

―――――――

In the wake of the Hamas–Israel conflict that exploded after October 7, 2023, major university presidents have demonstrated a willingness—or notable reticence—to speak out amid the anger expressed by faculty, students, alumni, and donors. The perfect storm of campus unrest has brought forth a new national debate—namely, how can universities support free speech principles during current turbulent times and beyond?

Renewed interest is being focused on the 1967 Kalven Report at the University of Chicago, which was updated in a 2014 report there by a Committee on Freedom of Expression chaired by Geoffrey R. Stone, the Edward H. Levi Distinguished Service Professor of Law.[1, 2]

Professor Stone is one of the nation's pre-eminent First Amendment scholars, and a former university provost. He has a unique vantage point for both the theory and practice of setting workable free speech boundaries on college campuses. In 2021, we discussed critical ideas that are now receiving increased national attention. Our conversation is especially useful to consider amid today's headlines and provides insights that will remain valuable as America enters its third century. It can help illuminate a pathway toward restoring free inquiry and free speech throughout higher education—articulating principles that are being tested almost daily as new expressive landmines appear.

Stuart Brotman: Let's talk about free speech in schools, including universities. I know you have been central in shaping thinking in this area,

chairing the committee at the University of Chicago, building upon
the work of one of your influencers, Harry Kalven, who had authored
a major report in this area a few decades earlier. What is your thinking
about how the First Amendment does or doesn't apply in the university context?

Geoffrey Stone: It's important to understand that the First Amendment
applies only to public institutions. The First Amendment applies to
the University of California or the University of Illinois, which are
public institutions, but it does not apply to the University of Chicago
or Harvard or Stanford, which are private institutions.

The First Amendment has no impact on the decision making or
autonomy of a private institution. So it's important to draw that distinction at the outset. On the other hand, even private universities
should aspire to promote free and open discourse and the questioning
and challenging of ideas. This is accepted wisdom for the intellectual
life of universities, in much the same way as the values embodied in
the First Amendment have come to be understood over time.

That's not true for all entities. Private corporations, for example,
don't have the same values and aspirations as a university.

But at the core of a university is the search for truth. At the core
of the university is the mission of seeking knowledge, seeking wisdom,
seeking insights that give us a better understanding of our society, of
science, and of culture.

In the same way that US Supreme Court Justices Holmes and
Brandeis argued that virtually unfettered speech helps to achieve truth
in the political arena, the best way to achieve truth in the academic
arena is not to have censorship but to have a broad and robust freedom of debate and discussion, and disagreement. So even in private
universities, there should be a commitment to free expression that is
very similar to what the First Amendment itself imposes on government entities.

What that means is that the institution should not suppress the
opportunity for students, faculty and other members of the university
community to explore ideas in ways that enable them to advocate for
what they see as wisdom, and to challenge what others may believe to
be wisdom and truth, and facts in order to seek greater knowledge.

That's the absolute core of the mission of a university, and it's very much at the core of the mission of the University of Chicago in particular, which from its very founding has been a leader in the pursuit of those values.

Brotman: Let's begin with the Kalven Report.

Stone: In 1967, the president of the University of Chicago, Edward Levi, appointed Harry Kalven to chair a committee to look at the extent to which a university should itself adopt positions on matters of public policy. This was during the height of the Vietnam War, and a large part of the issue was whether universities should weigh in on whether the Vietnam War was a good or bad thing. I must say, at roughly that time, I was arguing as a student in college, and later as a student at the University of Chicago Law School, that colleges and universities should take positions opposing the Vietnam War. I was wrong about that, but I believed that was true. I was within my rights to advocate for it, but it was the wrong position.

Brotman: And now?

Stone: I came to understand the Kalven Report, which was written at that time, took the position that the University of Chicago should not weigh in on matters of public policy unless those issues directly affect the university itself. But on matters of public policy, if the university takes positions, it would have a serious chilling effect on the willingness of faculty and students to take positions that are in opposition to what the university has declared to be "the right position." Therefore, the university should be extremely cautious about taking formal positions on matters of public policy.

I chaired the University of Chicago committee on free speech fifty years later. It had to do with the fact that at that time, at colleges and universities across the nation, it was increasingly the case that students and faculty members were demanding that universities disinvite speakers, or that speakers who had been invited should be silenced because the views that they would express would be opposed by the students or faculty as wrongheaded, inappropriate, and offensive. The challenge for universities was (and still is) to figure out whether certain speakers should be invited, or invited and then silenced, because members of the community oppose their views.

Brotman: What were the Stone Report's conclusions?

Stone: The University of Chicago adopted a statement that is three pages long. The first half of it discussed the history of the University of Chicago and gave examples of its own commitment to a robust protection of free speech.

Then the second part of it articulated an approach to free speech that basically says that free and open discourse is essential to the values and aspirations of a university and that a university therefore should not prohibit members of the community from inviting speakers who express views that others may find offensive.

Indeed, the report explained, it is the responsibility of the university affirmatively to protect the rights of students and faculty and other community members to speak themselves, or to invite speakers who would express views that others might find offensive. It should encourage students to listen to those views and to respond to the merits, to debate and to challenge those views if they disagree with them, but not to try to silence them, not to try to disrupt them, or to prevent them from having their say.

Brotman: How has this been received?

Stone: Interestingly, we wrote that report specifically for the University of Chicago. But several universities, beginning with Princeton, recognized that they could lop off the first half of the report, which talked about the history of the University of Chicago, and then adopt the second half of the report, which discussed the central principles. There are now some eighty colleges and universities across the country that have adopted what has come to be called the Chicago Principles. This is the standard that many institutions of higher education now embrace.

Brotman: And public universities?

Stone: Public universities have a different situation, because they are governed by the First Amendment. They do not have the freedom that a private university has, in theory, to reject those principles. So public universities have to conform strictly to what the First Amendment demands of them.

For the most part, that's what the Chicago Principles articulate: a public university, under the First Amendment, is responsible for allowing the expression by students, by faculty, and by visitors who are invited of views that may be disturbing or offensive to other members of the community, because they are subject to the basic principles of the First Amendment.

Brotman: How might this be limited in practice?

Stone: The commitment to free expression doesn't mean that in the classroom, say in a mathematics course, a student can start giving a speech about politics. There are constraints on the time, place, and manner of speech, which are permissible even, as illustrated by my example, on the content of speech in narrow circumstances, like the classroom.

Similarly, a commitment to free expression doesn't mean that professors cannot grade student papers or exams, based upon what the professor views as the wisdom or the excellence of the ideas that are being expressed.

The academic mission has within it a responsibility to teach and to evaluate scholarship. In so doing, one tries not to be ideological or political, but obviously the university and its faculty must make judgments about who to hire, who to promote, which students get A's, which students get B's, and so on.

But in the realm of public discourse in the university, the notion that the university, or its students or faculty, should have the authority to silence others because they don't like the views being expressed is incompatible with the First Amendment in a public university and incompatible with the core values and aspirations of a private university as well.

Brotman: California treats public and private universities the same, right?

Stone: The state of California has apparently said there's no real distinction between a public university and a private university in this respect. Private universities must act in accordance with the same standards that would apply to a public university.

Now this raises an interesting problem, because the private university has First Amendment rights to decide for itself what speech it wants or doesn't want to allow. A private university that seeks to achieve the goals and aspirations that I believe are essential to a true, well-functioning academic institution would itself choose to aspire to the same values that the First Amendment would apply to it.

But they don't have to do that. They have a First Amendment right to decide for themselves who they are. I think government laws that try to impose on private institutions obligations to comport with what the First Amendment would impose upon public institutions are making very difficult and delicate judgments about the academic freedom of a private institution.

Brotman: You seem firmly committed to the principle that universities should be silent when necessary.

Stone: Yes, I think the Kalven Report notion that universities themselves should not take official positions on political or other debates on public issues that do not directly affect the university is the proper stance. Because once a university goes down that road, it's very hard to say when to stop. Universities that declare certain ideas to be right or wrong will deter students and faculty members from challenging those ideas in a way that they should be free to do. It is simply not the business of a university to declare that abortion is wrong or that Trump was a bad president or that the war in Vietnam was a mistake. It is simply not the role of the university to take such positions except when such issues are directly related to the core functioning of the university itself.

It's not that I don't think there are right or wrong positions. But I don't think universities should take them, because they produce a chilling effect on the willingness of their students and their faculty to take counter positions. That's a dangerous thing in terms of the larger aspirations of a university community.

CHAPTER 5

Campuses Should Offer Teach-Ins on Freedom of Speech (2024)

With the academic year just a few short weeks away at college and university campuses nationwide, many are bracing for a reprise of last spring's ugly protests, encampments, and violent clashes among faculty, staff, and students.

Many administrators seemed like deer caught in headlights, unable or unwilling to acknowledge how serious the problem was at their institutions. Their feeble public responses made matters worse.

This led some college and university presidents to rehearse their testimonies when called before congressional subcommittees. Still others assumed the controversial role of mediators as they worked to reach settlements with those who had established illegal encampments and refused to vacate when requested.

In short, what seemed lost in the moment was the primary—and arguably most important—role that college and university presidents should play: that of educators. In an era where the notion of "teachable moments" are celebrated as a positive social good, the glaring lack of teachable moments here has been glaringly apparent. That needs to change.

It's high time for college and university presidents to reclaim their responsibilities as educators regarding the boundaries of freedom of speech—particularly when trespassing, property destruction, specific threats of violence, and outright violence are involved. Alas, too little attention has been devoted to articulating how the exercise of free speech—a cherished constitutional value—includes peaceful civil disobedience but excludes much of the destructive campus behavior that took place.

The Foundation for Individual Rights and Expression (FIRE) is a leading national nonprofit organization involved in First Amendment advocacy and research. In a FIRE survey conducted in conjunction with College Pulse last year, only 37 percent of students think it is never acceptable to shout down a speaker. Only 55 percent think blocking other students from hearing the speaker is unacceptable. And a growing number—27 percent in that survey—think violence can be an acceptable way to stop a campus speech.[1] These are alarming numbers.

Here's a practical and impactful step that can be implemented at various higher education institutions right before classes begin. Remember teach-ins? This educational format became popular in the 1960s, as campuses brought all students together to learn about threats to the environment on what became known as Earth Day. Other teach-ins soon became popular, including those regarding the Vietnam War.

According to Yale's Poorvu Center for Teaching and Learning, "Teach-ins empower students to learn about a specific topic or issue through multidisciplinary lenses and develop/evolve their perspectives by the end of the forum. . . . Teach-ins allow us to connect and discuss important issues as a campus community."[2]

Organizing a successful teach-in on freedom of speech needs to be approached thoughtfully and supported by necessary resources from various academic units. It will require organizing a range of speakers and a defined agenda. Community outreach will also be necessary.

One critical element should be considered. The college or university president should marshal all required support for a freedom of speech teach-in and have all activities coordinated directly from his or her office. That will send a strong signal about its importance.

The president (or the provost serving as the chief academic officer), as a well-informed moderator and visible institutional leader, should preside over the teach-in. The teach-in can be livestreamed and archived online to be viewed throughout the year, including by alumni and others unable to attend.

Ideally, a freedom of speech teach-in should be held on the same grounds where the prior campus demonstrations or encampments took place. Using these open campus spaces for a truly educational purpose may strike some as ironic. However, in the long run, it can help reassert the vital role of teaching in higher education that many have forgotten. This essential mission needs to be reasserted forthrightly since widespread lessons about the First Amendment and free expression are timely and necessary.

CHAPTER 6

Threats on Campuses Need to Be Dealt with Directly (2024)

The December 2023 explosive congressional hearing with presidents from among some of the nation's most elite universities—Harvard, MIT, and the University of Pennsylvania—nearly broke the internet. All three academic leaders could not clearly state that advocating genocide against Jews might violate their campus codes of conduct. Politicians of all stripes—along with students, faculty, alumni, and prominent donors—were shocked that what seemed like something defined by a bright line of morality would be portrayed as requiring nuance in response.

Elizabeth Magill, Penn's president, created the most memorable soundbite while under intense questioning by Rep. Elise Stefanik, (R-NY). When asked by Stefanik whether calling for the genocide of Jews constituted bullying or harassment, Magill soberly replied, "It is a context-dependent decision, congresswoman."

Within twenty-four hours, she issued an apologetic video for misspeaking under pressure, but that did not prove to be enough to mitigate the damage by not responding affirmatively. The Penn Board of Trustees accepted her resignation by the end of the week, along with that of its chair, Scott Bok.

Although this controversy has been framed as a debate about protecting the First Amendment and free speech values on campus, more focus needs to be made on the actual legal standard that would be applied to the context-dependent decision that Magill indicated would be necessary to consider. Penn, a private university, isn't covered by the

First Amendment, which deals with restrictions on free speech by state actors. Nevertheless, it models its campus code of conduct on the same constitutional principles applicable here.

There is a new Supreme Court precedent, established by *Counterman v. Colorado*, that underscores why Magill's assertion could not be supported as a matter of law.[1] When chants of "Kill the Jews" are made during demonstrations on Penn's campus or elsewhere, they would not be considered as just angry words but rather as "true threats." Consequently, like other expressive categories such as child pornography or obscenity, they would not be covered by the free speech protection of the First Amendment or by any university code of conduct that references it as a benchmark.

The central legal issue is whether this phrase (or others, such as "Intifada" or "From the river to the sea, Palestine will be free") constitutes a threat that may be punished by a university. The Supreme Court has indicated that the speaker need not actually intend to carry out the threat. Rather, all that must be proven is that the speaker intended to communicate a threat.

Not surprisingly, over the last twenty years, lower federal appellate courts have not followed a uniform standard about what level of intention was needed to distinguish a genuine threat from protected free speech. That's why the court's decision in *Counterman v. Colorado* is so important. The court finally adopted a rule that speech is not protected if the speaker "consciously disregarded a substantial risk that his communications would be viewed as threatening violence."

This subjective standard now has been set at a level of "recklessness" on behalf of the speaker, which is a lower threshold than establishing an intent to harm or knowing that the communication would do harm.

Anyone who defaces campus property with a "Kill the Jews" slogan or leads the chanting of this type of mantra in a public demonstration would be consciously assuming the risk that these words would be threatening violence. Under the *Counterman* decision, these words clearly are meant to threaten violence (and, in some cases, have been accompanied by physical assaults on nearby individuals identified as Jews, too).

This means that Magill's response (along with similar ones by Harvard's Claudine Gay and MIT's Sally Kornbluth) was wrong on both moral and legal grounds. There is no way to contextualize genocidal expressions against Jews as anything other than bullying or harassing threats of violence. They are clearly actual threats—not free speech—and must be dealt with accordingly.

CHAPTER 7

Stanford Law's Free Speech Teachable Moments (2023)

————

I am a lawyer, First Amendment scholar, and a tenured journalism and media professor at a major research university. Given these multiple professional identities, my thoughts on a recent headline-grabbing incident at Stanford Law School cannot be summarized by a pithy tweet, which is the coin of the realm in the social media world.

A Stanford Law event sponsored by its Federalist Society, a conservative and libertarian legal organization, has received widespread national media attention for the chaos it caused in real time—and more importantly, the threat to free speech that it represents.

The March 2023 event titled, "The Fifth Circuit in Conversation with the Supreme Court: COVID, Guns, and Twitter," involved a packed auditorium of Stanford Law students, including a hundred protesters who showed up to loudly interrupt the invited speaker, Judge Stuart Kyle Duncan of the 5th US Circuit Court of Appeals at New Orleans.

Judge Duncan is a noted conservative jurist who has expressed views, both before and after his appointment by President Donald Trump to the federal bench in 2018, that these students found to be contrary to their strongly held political and moral beliefs on issues such as same-sex marriage and transgender rights.

Loudly voiced opposition from protesters was a classic "heckler's veto" (first coined by the late University of Chicago Law Professor Harry Kalven)—silencing a speaker with whom they disagreed by shouting him down—hoping that this would be enough to have Judge

25

Duncan walk away. But this didn't succeed in full, as Judge Duncan remained at the podium to answer questions from the students in lieu of the prepared remarks he had planned to deliver.

While this shout-down at Stanford Law provided a media-ready, dramatic, and emotionally charged campus event, the media's response to it similarly spun out of control. By now, the initial story has been written and circulated widely. But there needs to be greater attention in the media and legal communities, focusing on larger issues at play: both public discourse and trust in the judiciary are suffering.

Stanford Law Dean Jenny S. Martinez wisely recognized that what happened at her esteemed institution provided a teachable moment. Her ten-page letter on March 22 to the Stanford Law community reflected well on both her as the school's leader and on her under-standing of legal free speech precedents and values.[1]

In the letter, she took care to differentiate forums and circum-stances in which free speech is protected, citing extensive legal prece-dent. She also noted that the First Amendment bars regulating speech "on the ground that listeners might find its content disturbing."

"There is temptation to a system in which people holding views perceived by some as harmful or offensive are not allowed to speak, to avoid giving legitimacy to their views or upsetting members of the com-munity, but history teaches us that this is a temptation to be avoided," Martinez wrote. "I believe that strong protection for freedom of speech is a bedrock principle that ultimately supports diversity, equity and inclusion, and that we must do everything in our power to ensure that it endures."

Dean Martinez backed up her words in the letter by announcing mandatory educational programming for all Stanford Law students in the coming weeks, focusing on freedom of speech and the norms of the legal profession.

Along with Stanford University President Marc Tessier-Lavigne, Dean Martinez also formally apologized to Judge Duncan in a separate letter: ". . . to acknowledge that his speech was disrupted in ways that undermine his ability to deliver the remarks he wanted to give to audi-ence members who wanted to hear them, as a result of the failure to ensure that the university's disruption policies were followed."[2]

The lessons from this event reach well beyond campus settings. In recent years, respect for the US Supreme Court—and the federal judiciary as a whole—has experienced a steep decline among the public at large, according to Gallup, a well-respected national survey firm.

Even before the Supreme Court overturned its long-standing constitutional protection for abortion in *Dobbs v. Jackson Women's Health Organization*, Gallup found that in 2022, only 25 percent of US adults had "a great deal" or "quite a lot of confidence" in the Supreme Court. And for the federal judiciary, a separate 2022 Gallup survey found that trust in the judicial branch had "cratered" since 2020, with less than half of US adults conveying such trust—the first time this has happened since Gallup began surveys in this area in 1972.[3]

At the Stanford Law event, according to a March 10 article from *Original Jurisdiction*, a Substack by legal journalist David Lat, Judge Duncan reportedly used his smartphone to record the student protesters, leading one observer to note that he looked "more like a YouTuber storming the Capitol than a federal judge coming to speak." He taunted the students by calling them "juvenile idiots," noting that the "prisoners were now running the asylum."[4]

It's highly unlikely that Judge Duncan would have acted or spoken this way while hearing any cases. His behavior at the event, even though provoked into angry name-calling, will not help the growing perception that federal judges are no longer neutral arbiters, but rather just another group of political combatants in a nation deeply divided into red and blue mindsets.

Perhaps Judge Duncan and his peers would be well advised to review Dean Martinez's more generalized wisdom. "Naming perceived harm, exploring it, and debating solutions with people who disagree about the nature and fact of the harm or the correct solutions are the very essence of legal work," Martinez wrote in her letter to the law school community.

"Lively, candid, civil, and evidence-based discourse in disagreement is not just positive for our community, constituted as it is in difference, it is a professional duty," she wrote. "Observance of this duty matters most, not least, when we are convinced that others haven't."

Put simply, our faith in the rule of law may depend upon judges who are committed to always meet this high standard. As a lawyer, and as an American citizen who strongly supports our democratic institutions, I recognize how important it is to reverse the troubling trend of declining confidence in our judicial branch.

And in all my professional identities, I welcome more media coverage that helps foster further discussion about greater respect for free speech values on college campuses and supports judges in following the example of Stanford Law Dean Martinez—so they can better reflect their positions of leadership in the legal community and society at large.

CHAPTER 8

Explicitly Addressing College Self-Censorship in the New Academic Year (2023)

With the beginning of the college academic year, those of us teaching this fall are drafting various course syllabi—seeing what might be worth revisiting, such as new readings that might be added.

But all too often, the upfront syllabus boilerplate sections are overlooked since they are cut and pasted from previous versions of the same course or similar ones. Unfortunately, a section dealing with free expression in the classroom is missing in many.

This is a more focused area than campus speech, which continues to attract national headlines as outside speakers from the Right and Left are disinvited or shouted down. The issue here is less about censorship—which may be referenced in a syllabus by linking to an established campuswide free-expression policy or the University of Chicago Principles adopted by dozens of universities—and more about self-censorship. The latter concern often is more difficult to identify since it involves an unwillingness to speak freely, considering actual or perceived consequences for doing so. Data and personal experience suggest this needs to be addressed head-on.

For example, the Heterodox Academy's Campus Expression Survey asked more than 1,500 full-time college students from universities across the country about their reluctance to share their views on various topics in class and what variables are associated with this reluctance.[1] Just over 58 percent of the respondents said they were reluctant to share their views on politics, race, sexual orientation, gender or religion in the classroom.

I concur with the observation of Nicole Barbaro, the organization's director of communications and marketing. "This is a real problem that should concern all educators, especially across the social sciences, biological sciences, and humanities, where these topics are most likely to be central to academic research and discussions. If students are not comfortable talking about these topics in class—a space intended for exploring ideas, discussing research and critically thinking about problems—then our universities are, in part, failing at their intended purpose."[2]

Classroom self-censorship is a two-sided phenomenon. The Foundation for Individual Rights and Expression (FIRE) surveyed almost fifteen hundred college faculty members nationwide to dig deeper into the issue. Its data shows that a third of faculty (34 percent) reported that they self-censor on campus "fairly" or "very" often. According to FIRE, faculty members are more likely to self-censor today than during the Joseph McCarthy era of the 1950s.[3]

Based on its survey, this observation again rings true to me and probably to countless other faculty members. "It is hard to comprehend the fact that the very group of people charged to showcase how viewpoint diversity and healthy debate functions are themselves limiting their expression—at rates higher than the students they are supposed to teach."[4]

Ten years ago, I served as the inaugural professor of communication in residence at Northwestern University in Qatar. Unlike the United States, there was no First Amendment to reference there. My students were brought up in a culture where free speech was not encouraged and, in fact, could be punished severely as a matter of law.

By discussing self-censorship in class with my students at the outset, I was gratified by how an explicit conversation at the beginning of the semester—supported and reinforced with each class session—produced a high level of viewpoint diversity and dissenting voices. I saw how the students felt free to engage with me in covering the course material, not just learning about free expression as an ideal but also experiencing it in practice.

Given the wave of classroom self-censorship that has hit US college classrooms in the intervening years, I intend not just to discuss this when I provide a course overview but also explicitly remove classroom self-censorship guardrails that may exist, even if they are not acknowledged. The course syllabus is the ideal place to convey this, especially since it will be referenced by the students continuously throughout the semester.

CHAPTER 9

Exploring Campus "Zero Tolerance" to Combat Antisemitism (2024)

The presidents of three of America's most elite universities—Harvard, MIT, and the University of Pennsylvania—were the subject of glaring national attention while appearing before the House Committee on Education and the Workforce. Under pointed questioning by Representative Elise Stefanik (R-NY), all three prominent academic leaders failed to articulate simply whether advocating genocide against Jews would constitute a violation of their campus conduct codes. The need for responding with moral clarity, combined with the absence of any concrete policy in place that any of them could mention, created the proverbial perfect storm. Both Harvard's President Claudine Gay and Penn's President Elizabeth Magill resigned in its wake.

But that event also presents a larger opportunity to discuss what reasonable measures could be adopted by higher education institutions writ large as they confront the reality of combating the alarming rise of antisemitism and growing threats to Jewish students and faculty. Alas, the path forward may not be found in the hallowed halls of ivy, but rather in the sagebrush of Killeen, Texas. That's where Central Texas College (CTC) is located, and where discussing the possibilities of a "zero tolerance policy" for universities should begin.

There, the concern is more about consequences than context. As part of its "zero tolerance policy," CTC has in place procedures for "appropriate disciplinary action for every weapon, threat, incident of hazing, stalking, harassment or discrimination, sexual misconduct, and/ or violent act that is reasonably substantiated through investigation."[1]

The entire campus community has been put on notice; the text of the policy puts it in plain language. "A zero tolerance policy is one that requires an appropriate penalty be imposed based on the individual circumstances. It is, as it states, intolerant of the prohibited behavior."

Further, CTC has indicated that it "may also take disciplinary action for certain violations reported off campus to the extent these violations may have an impact on the campus. This includes but is not limited to violations that pose an ongoing danger to students or may cause harm to the campus community, including violent crimes, hate crimes, disturbing or threatening actions, and illegal conduct."

Among the inappropriate behaviors CTC notes are "verbal, written, or acts of harassment/discrimination to include sexual harassment/discrimination, stalking, and bullying; acts or actions which can be interpreted as physical assault; hazing or dangerous initiations; threats or actions to harm someone or endanger the safety of others; behaviors or actions interpreted by a reasonable person as having potential for violence and/or acts of aggression; and threats to destroy or the actual destruction of property."

What would happen if academic leaders around the country began to consider adopting a comparable zero tolerance policy on campus to concretely address how they would respond to the next calls for genocide against Jews? And beyond that, what if they were prepared to back up their words with the actions CTC expressed it is willing to take? "Violators will be subject to appropriate discipline up to and including termination, expulsion, and arrest."

Considering such an approach would help the clouds to clear and rays of light to begin shining through once again. New thinking is needed to directly confront the antisemitic dangers that are so apparent now on college campuses nationwide. Zero tolerance is a useful way to start the conversation about what needs to be done—not in theory, but in practice.

PART III
DIGITAL TRANSFORMATION

New challenges continue to emerge online: artificial intelligence-generated content, virtual reality experiences, and forms of digital communication we haven't yet imagined. Will it be possible to create a durable foundation for protecting free expression rights regardless of how technology evolves?

CHAPTER 10

Why the Internet Stays Free (2025)

The Case That Changed Everything

In the landmark 1997 Supreme Court case, *Reno v. American Civil Liberties Union*, the Court struck down a federal law that would have heavily restricted online speech, ruling unanimously that the internet deserved the strongest possible free speech protections under the First Amendment. This foundational decision fundamentally shaped how we use the internet today.

At the time of this ruling, only about forty million Americans used the internet—compared to over 275 million today. Most people were still using dial-up modems, and social media didn't exist. Yet the Court's decision has proven remarkably durable, continuing to protect our online freedoms even as technology has transformed society beyond recognition.

This case matters because it established a simple but powerful principle: the government cannot censor online speech just because some people might find it offensive or inappropriate. Unlike television and radio, which face regulatory content restrictions, the internet operates under the same free speech rules as newspapers, books, and face-to-face conversations.

What Made the Internet Different

Justice John Paul Stevens, who wrote the Court's opinion, understood that the internet was unlike any communication medium that had come before. He noted several key differences that justified stronger constitutional protection:[1]

Space Without Limits: Unlike radio and TV, which are limited by available broadcast frequencies, the internet offers unlimited space for communication. There's room for everyone to speak without crowding out others.

Active Choice, Not Passive Reception: When you watch TV or listen to the radio, content comes to you automatically. Online, you must actively seek out content by typing in web addresses, clicking links, or downloading apps. This makes "accidental" exposure to unwanted material much less likely.

Not Really Free: Despite appearances, internet access requires payment—whether through monthly service fees or app subscriptions. This distinguishes it from broadcast television and radio, which anyone can access for free.

Global Reach: The internet connects people across national boundaries in ways that traditional media cannot, making local content regulation practically impossible and constitutionally problematic.

Why Some Think the Rules Should Change

As the internet has evolved, some critics argue that this landmark decision no longer makes sense. They point to several changes:

- **Mobile Access**: Smartphones and tablets make internet content as accessible as turning on a radio.
- **Free Wi-Fi**: Public internet access is now widely available without direct payment.
- **Social Media Algorithms**: Platforms now push content to users rather than requiring active searching.
- **Children Online**: Kids can now access inappropriate material more easily than ever before.

These critics suggest that since the internet now looks more like traditional broadcasting—widely accessible and sometimes passively consumed—it should face similar government content restrictions.

Why the Decision Still Makes Sense

However, these technological changes strengthen the case for keeping the internet free rather than weakening it. Here's why:

The Core Structure Hasn't Changed: The internet still operates on the same basic principle it did when this landmark case was decided—users must take active steps to access specific content. Even with smartphones and social media, you still must choose which apps to download, which accounts to follow, and which links to click.

More Speech, Not Less: The explosion of online content since this ruling has proven the Court's point about the benefits of unlimited communicative space. Billions of people can now publish content without displacing others—something impossible with traditional broadcasting.

Global Communication: The internet's international nature has only intensified since this landmark ruling, making local content regulation even more problematic and constitutionally questionable.

User Control: Modern internet users have more control over their online experience than users did when this case was decided, with sophisticated filtering tools, parental controls, and content warnings widely available.

The Broadcasting Comparison: Why It Doesn't Work

The Supreme Court treats television and radio differently from other forms of communication, allowing more government regulation of broadcast content. The Court has justified these restrictions because broadcasting has unique characteristics:

- Limited space (only so many frequencies available)

- Passive reception (content comes to you automatically)
- Universal accessibility (free to anyone with a radio or TV)
- Easy access by children (kids can turn on devices without adult supervision)

None of these characteristics truly applies to the internet. Even with mobile devices and free Wi-Fi, internet use requires more active engagement than broadcast consumption. Users must navigate to specific sites and apps, choose content, and can easily avoid material they don't want to see.

Online Activities, Democratic Values

The internet has become "a public square, a library, a doctor's office, a shop, a school, a design studio, an office, a cinema, a bank, and so much more."[2] It serves as the primary place where Americans get news, debate politics, share ideas, and participate in democratic life.

Weakening constitutional protection for online speech would fundamentally alter this multifaceted communication platform. Government officials could potentially restrict online political criticism, ban controversial scientific discussions, or limit access to information that challenges official viewpoints.

The Supreme Court decision reflected the wisdom to recognize that the internet's unique characteristics—its unlimited capacity, global reach, and requirement for active user engagement—make it fundamentally different from traditional broadcast media. These characteristics have only become more pronounced as technology has advanced.

CHAPTER 11

First Amendment Rights Hit Turbulence in Cyberspace (2016)

Political leaders and citizens alike are paying greater attention to the nature of democracy in a market economy. Age-old questions of political philosophy are being articulated once again: What is the role of government compared to the rights of its citizens? What are the responsibilities of a society with respect to its less fortunate members? What are a citizen's duties to the broader community?

Superimposed on this set of political questions is the reality of our information society—the massive outpouring of information and communications into virtually all our common activities.

Originally, this was accompanied by an Orwellian fear of government oppression through advanced technology, or conversely, as Neil Postman later warned, the nightmare of "amusing ourselves to death" via television. More recently, a sense of online euphoria seemed to dominate, as we marveled at the internet's instantaneous connections to information and other interested souls around the world.

Yet even the internet's most ardent enthusiasts warn of privacy threats, acknowledge potential social inequities, and underscore the importance of continuous learning and adaptation in a world of rapid change.

Regardless of perspective, however, there appears to be a looming anxiety about our digital age: distrust of traditional authority, concern about the expanse of government, and, at the same time, a search for meaning and connection to our broader society. In this uncertain political climate, accentuated by advancing and rapidly changing technology, it is important to return to "first principles" that serve as the foundation for our constitutional values of free expression.

The Four Pillars of Free Expression

Thomas Emerson's classic work, *The System of Freedom of Expression*, summarized four core values of free expression that are reflected in the First Amendment. These principles, developed centuries ago, remain surprisingly relevant in our digital age.

The first value, borrowing from political philosopher Alexander Meiklejohn, is the participation in self-government that freedom of speech makes possible—and without which democracy cannot function. Every tweet, every Facebook post, every online petition represents this principle in action.

From John Stuart Mill's famous essay "On Liberty," along with the writings of many others, came a second value—that a free and unfettered marketplace of ideas is the best way to search for truth. This isn't because truth will always prevail over falsehood, as John Milton alleged in his famous "Areopagitica," but because there's ordinarily a better chance of approximating truth when ideas are challenged by competing ideas than when they're accepted dogmatically.

Emerson's third value is self-expression—the opportunity the First Amendment provides for individuals to say what's on their mind and express their creativity through literature, science, art, music, and now, digital media.

The fourth value is what Emerson called catharsis and the consequent maintenance of balance in society between stability and change. By letting people blow off steam, a society preserves its equilibrium in the short run. Equally important, this pressure valve heightens awareness of problems that need to be addressed if stability is to be sustained in the long run.

The Digital Challenge

An important civic dialogue about the internet that we need to be pursuing is how best to reaffirm our constitutional values of free expression in cyberspace. Lawyers and technologists have dominated the conversation to date, but the disciplinary boundaries need to be expanded. We need philosophers, historians, sociologists, and others in core liberal arts fields to become engaged, along with our diverse body politic.

These values need to be reflected as a public good—not just for the town square, but for the digital domain as well. The internet has become our new public forum, and the principles that have guided American democracy for over two centuries must guide us through the unprecedented digital revolution.

Bans on Social Media and Elsewhere Raise Free Expression Red Flags (2022)

Elon Musk, Twitter's new owner, decided to lift a nearly three-year ban that had been imposed on Donald Trump during the final days of his presidency. Musk indicated this reversal represented "the will of the people," based on a quick, unscientific online poll he posted that showed a slim majority approved of the former president being allowed back on Twitter to reach the eighty-eight million people who had been his followers at the time of his banishment.

Regardless of one's feelings about Musk or Trump or what they stand for, this move does not raise any actual First Amendment concerns. Twitter is not owned or operated by any governmental entity, so at no time has there been government involvement in deciding whether to exclude or include Trump.

His most fervent supporters and most vocal detractors have the freedom to discuss this matter on Twitter for as long as they wish. Some may sign up for new verified Twitter accounts Musk has launched, while others may decide to move on to other social media platforms. In other words, this event really doesn't implicate the First Amendment in a legal sense or violate its broader free speech values.

When Government Really Crosses the Line

In contrast, Trump's potential rival for the Republican nomination has rightfully been called out for violating the First Amendment and free speech values more directly. Last month, US District Chief

Judge Mark Walker issued a 138-page opinion that prevented Florida from implementing new legislation strongly supported by Gov. Ron DeSantis, who signed it into law with a full blast of media exposure earlier this year.

This "anti-woke" legislation, known as the Individual Freedom Act, is designed to prohibit schools and companies from making students and employees feel guilt or blame based on race or sex. It indicates that a person should not be instructed to "feel guilt, anguish, or any other form of psychological distress" due to their race, color, sex, or national origin.

But the law is not as benign as this description may imply. It also contains troublesome provisions that would apply to all public institutions of higher learning in Florida. "The law officially bans professors from expressing disfavored viewpoints in university classrooms while permitting unfettered expression of the opposite viewpoints," wrote Judge Walker. "Defendants argue that, under this Act, professors enjoy 'academic freedom' so long as they express only those viewpoints of which the State approves. This is positively dystopian."[1]

Although Florida vowed to appeal this ruling, the judge's powerful language reminds us that there still are strong forces within government that want to restrict free speech in clear violation of the First Amendment. The Florida Legislature, backed by DeSantis, represents the very type of government intrusion that is prohibited by the First Amendment.

The Real Threat to Free Speech

The white noise about Trump's potential reemergence on Twitter continues, even though he has started his own social media platform, Truth Social, as a competitor. But we all would be much better served by resisting the Florida legislation and any of its offspring that may rise in other states.

As Judge Walker wrote, "The powers in charge of Florida's public university system have declared the State has unfettered authority to muzzle its professors in the name of 'freedom.'" And with a literary flourish, he noted George Orwell's doomsday novel *1984* as a close analogy of this law's potential consequences.

With greater attention to how the First Amendment affects our everyday lives, Americans of all ideologies should express their opinions about these headline-making free speech developments—whether on Twitter or anywhere else. The platform may change, but the principles remain the same.

CHAPTER 12

The TikTok Saga—National Security vs. Free Expression (2025)

TikTok's ownership has become a real-world test of whether America's free expression protections can survive in the digital age. While a deal now appears imminent, the way we've handled this crisis reveals troubling gaps in how our democracy protects the communication rights of millions of Americans.

What Actually Happened

For almost a year now, 170 million Americans have been caught in limbo, unsure whether they'll be able to keep using their favorite social media app. The ban took effect after ByteDance, the China-based parent company of TikTok, refused to sell the service before the deadline of the Protecting Americans from Foreign Adversary Controlled Applications Act (PAFACA). But here's the twist: the ban has yet to be enforced.

Instead, we've watched an unprecedented constitutional drama unfold. TikTok voluntarily suspended its services in the United States on January 18, 2025, the day before the deadline of the law, even though President Joe Biden had declined to enforce the ban on his last day in office. The app came back the next day when Trump signaled he would delay enforcement.

Since then, Trump has extended the deadline four times—first to April 5, then to June 19, then to September 17, and most recently to December 16, 2025. Each extension has been accompanied by extraordinary claims about presidential power that have legal experts worried.

The Deal That's Finally Taking Shape

A deal has been reached between the Trump administration and China to keep TikTok operational in the United States, administration officials announced on September 15, 2025. President Donald Trump signed an executive order approving a proposal that would keep TikTok alive in the US in a transaction that Vice President JD Vance said values the business at $14 billion.

Here's how the deal works: a consortium of investors, including Oracle, Silver Lake, and Andreessen Horowitz, may oversee TikTok's US operations. These investors are expected to hold an 80 percent stake, and the remaining shares will belong to Chinese stakeholders. The new venture will get a copy of TikTok's most valuable asset, its content recommendation algorithm, which will then be retrained on US data.

When Congress passed the TikTok ban with overwhelming support from both parties, it made the most significant restriction on a communications platform in American history. Think about it: 170 million Americans suddenly faced losing their primary way to share videos, follow creators, and discover content.

This isn't just about one app. It's about a fundamental question: Can the government shut down entire platforms where Americans communicate? The First Amendment has traditionally said no—that government can't engage in "prior restraint," which means stopping speech before it happens rather than punishing illegal speech afterward.

Imagine if the government could shut down entire newspapers because it didn't like who owned them, rather than addressing specific harmful content. That's essentially what's happening here, but in the digital age.

The Constitutional Crisis Nobody's Talking About

The most troubling part isn't the ban itself; it's how it's been handled.

According to Harvard Law School professor Jack Goldsmith, "the president and the attorney general have asserted a power to wipe out the effects of any law related to national security or foreign affairs on the president's say so," an assertion that is "maybe the broadest I have ever seen any president or Justice Department make, ever, in any context."[1]

What this means in plain English: If a president can indefinitely ignore laws passed by Congress by claiming national security, what other rights might be suspended the same way?

The National Security vs. Free Expression Dilemma

The government's concerns aren't imaginary. Officials worry that laws in China require Chinese companies to hand over data requested by the government, and there are legitimate questions about the proprietary algorithm that populates what users see on the app.

But here's the First Amendment problem: The ban doesn't target specific harmful content or data practices. Instead, it eliminates an entire communication platform used by millions of Americans for everything from political debate to artistic expression to business promotion.

The Constitution typically requires the government to use the least restrictive means possible to address problems. Could data security requirements, oversight mechanisms, or transparency mandates achieve the same security goals without shutting down a major forum for American expression?

What Makes This Different

TikTok has become what the Supreme Court calls "the modern public square"—a place where citizens gather to exchange ideas and debate issues. For millions of Americans, especially young people, it's their primary source of news and their main platform for creative expression.

The government argues that foreign ownership makes TikTok different, but this reasoning conflicts with basic free expression principles. Americans have the right to receive information regardless of where it comes from. The First Amendment protects our right to hear foreign perspectives, read international news, and engage with global communities.

The Dangerous Precedents We're Setting

Whatever happens with TikTok, this controversy has already established troubling precedents:

Executive Power Over Speech: The pattern of congressional action followed by presidential delays creates uncertainty about who really controls free speech policy in America.

Platforms as Diplomatic Tools: When communication platforms become bargaining chips in international negotiations, it signals that American free speech rights can be subject to geopolitical leverage.

National Security Trumps Speech: The resolution will either show that the government must carefully balance security and speech concerns or demonstrate that political considerations can override First Amendment protections when it's convenient.

The Real Test Ahead

The proposed deal may solve the immediate TikTok problem, but it doesn't address the underlying constitutional issues.

Even if this deal works, what happens next time? What if the government decides another platform poses security risks? Will we go through another year of constitutional uncertainty while millions of Americans wonder if their primary communication tool will disappear?

The TikTok saga reveals a fundamental problem. Our constitutional system wasn't designed for an age when expression happens on global digital platforms that can be switched off by government decree. The framers of the First Amendment couldn't have imagined these platforms, which simultaneously function as private businesses, public forums, and strategic infrastructure.

The Path Forward

Future digital governance needs to preserve First Amendment principles while acknowledging new realities:

Clearer Rules: We need transparent criteria for when national security can override free speech considerations, not ad hoc political decisions that leave citizens uncertain about their rights.

Proportional Responses: Regulatory tools must be sophisticated enough to address specific risks without eliminating entire forums for expression.

Democratic Process: Decisions affecting Americans' free speech rights should be made through deliberative democratic processes, not executive orders or international negotiations.

Constitutional Consistency: First Amendment principles should apply consistently across digital platforms, regardless of their ownership or political convenience.

The Uncomfortable Truth

The spectacle of repeated presidential delays of congressionally mandated enforcement has created a constitutional gray area that threatens core principles of free expression. When executive power can indefinitely postpone legislative mandates through procedural extensions, what does that mean for the constitutional rights of millions of Americans?

How do we protect free expression in an age when communication happens on platforms that exist at the intersection of technology, national security, and international relations? That's the real test at hand. It is not just keeping one app alive, but building a framework for digital governance that preserves the free expression principles our democracy depends on. The TikTok saga is just the beginning.

CHAPTER 13

Elon Musk's Digital Town Square Model for Twitter (Now X) Remains Elusive (2023)

When Elon Musk acquired Twitter in 2023, he sent a prominent virtue signal. Musk indicated that under his ownership, Twitter would be "a common digital town square, where a wide range of beliefs can be debated in a healthy manner."

This notion was quickly picked up in numerous glowing tweets, then amplified by media worldwide. But we have learned in the ensuing months that there never was and never will be a true digital town square.

The Analog Inspiration

Let's begin by reviewing the analog version of what Musk imagined. The Speakers' Corner in London's Hyde Park is the model that is widely cited. It's a section of the park, near Marble Arch, that enables individuals from a wide range of ideologies—mainstream to fringe—to express their views in the open air for all within earshot to hear.

Speakers' Corner often is used as an example to demonstrate robust freedom of speech. Anyone can appear unannounced and talk on almost any subject. Counter-speech in the form of heckling is permitted and common, particularly by those who congregate there regularly. And for more than a century, those who used it to express their opinions have included Karl Marx and George Orwell.

It's not the free-for-all that one might envision, however. Since the space is sanctioned by the government on public property, Speakers' Corner remains under careful watch. In fact, speaking there confers no immunity from the law. In practice, the police intervene with speakers when they receive complaints.

Why the Digital Version Falls Short

Social media platforms such as Twitter are private enterprises with extensive service terms that require user agreements. In some cases, an additional layer of verification may be required to confirm identity. These factors make them fundamentally different from Speakers' Corner or public spaces that are open to all comers.

True, Twitter and its peers reflect a wide range of beliefs, but few regular users would confirm that these are debated "in a healthy manner." United Kingdom law, like US law, recognizes that freedom of speech should not be limited to the inoffensive. Rather, it should extend to "the irritating, the contentious, the eccentric, the heretical, the unwelcome, and the provocative"—provided such speech doesn't tend to provoke violence.[1]

Despite the breakdown of Musk's digital town square metaphor when analyzed more closely, there continues to be a need for content moderation on Twitter under his watch, just as there is at Speakers' Corner. How much content moderation is designed and implemented (or not) seems to be the more appropriate way to assess whether a "digital town square" can move from idealistic rhetoric to reality while still preserving the open expressive values that remain a cherished social good.

The Ongoing Challenge

The dream of a truly open digital forum where all ideas can compete freely remains compelling. But the reality is that any platform—whether physical or digital—requires some level of oversight to prevent it from becoming unusable. The challenge isn't eliminating moderation, but creating transparent, fair systems that protect both free expression and user safety.

Musk's experiment continues, and with it, our ongoing education about the complexities of digital free speech in the modern age.

CHAPTER 14

Creating an Internet Fairness Doctrine Would Backfire (2020)

President Trump issued an "Executive Order on Preventing Online Censorship" stating that the protections conferred by Section 230 of the 1996 Communications Decency Act should be "clarified." Among other things, the order called on the Department of Justice to "assess whether any online platforms are problematic vehicles for government speech due to viewpoint discrimination."

This suggests a view that private entities should be compelled to serve as viewpoint-neutral vehicles for the dissemination of "government speech." Senator Josh Hawley (R-MO) introduced legislation that would have amended Section 230 so that "Big tech companies would have to prove to the FTC by clear and convincing evidence that their algorithms and content-removal practices are politically neutral."[1]

This regulatory push comes as part of a broader attack on Section 230, the foundational statute that protects internet companies from being liable for content posted by third parties. If your neighbor sends a tweet asserting that you are a bank robber, you could pursue a defamation claim against the neighbor but not against Twitter. The fact that Twitter didn't preemptively detect and block the defamatory tweet wouldn't saddle Twitter with any legal liability.

Lessons from the Original Fairness Doctrine

For much of the second half of the twentieth century, US broadcasters operated under the FCC's "fairness doctrine," which required them to

53

present a balanced range of perspectives on issues of public interest. The FCC successfully defended the doctrine's constitutionality in *Red Lion Broadcasting Co., Inc. v. FCC*, a landmark 1969 Supreme Court decision. "It does not violate the First Amendment," the Court wrote, "to treat licensees given the privilege of using scarce radio frequencies as proxies for the entire community, obligated to give suitable time and attention to matters of great public concern."[2]

But by the mid-1980s, both the broadcasting landscape and the FCC's views had changed. Growth in the number of television and radio stations meant that the scarcity cited by the Supreme Court in *Red Lion Broadcasting* was no longer a concern. The FCC's own general counsel concluded that the rules intended to enforce fairness were "no longer necessary to achieve diversity of viewpoint."

In 1987, the FCC commissioners voted unanimously to abolish the fairness doctrine. As its chairman explained, "We seek to extend to the electronic press the same First Amendment guarantees that the print media have enjoyed since our country's inception."

Why the Internet Is Different

Today, thanks to the internet, the number of sources from which people can access information is limitless. While many legitimate criticisms can be leveled at today's internet ecosystem, a lack of opportunity to access a diverse range of information sources and viewpoints is not one of them.

That's a good reason why the recent trend to push for regulation that would attempt to bring back something resembling the fairness doctrine for online content is more concerning. As private entities, social media companies are not bound by the First Amendment, which constrains the government from "abridging the freedom of speech."

Ironically, if the government were to enact what amounts to an internet fairness doctrine to force large social media companies to be "politically neutral"—however that might be defined—that itself would be a violation of the First Amendment.

The Constitutional Problem

Even in its mid-twentieth-century heyday, the fairness doctrine was constitutionally suspect, as it purported to leave in government hands the power to decide what constituted balanced coverage of issues of public interest by private broadcasters. It only survived Supreme Court review in the 1960s because the limited number of available television and radio stations gave rise to concerns that the public might be denied access to multiple viewpoints.

Under the First Amendment, each social media platform or other privately-operated website is free to welcome a diverse range of viewpoints or to preferentially welcome viewpoints from either the political right or the political left. And while there are plenty of internet sites that individually offer a politically narrow set of perspectives, the internet certainly doesn't prevent users from accessing multiple viewpoints.

A Healthier Internet Without Government Control

We now live in a world with a level of diversity of information sources that would have been incomprehensible three decades ago. Of course, for all the benefits of the contemporary online environment, there's also plenty not to like, including toxicity, misinformation and disinformation, and the use of the internet for criminal purposes.

We can and should seek solutions to build a healthier, safer internet. But those solutions should not include—and under the First Amendment, cannot include—vastly increased state control over the online information ecosystem through punishment of internet companies not meeting the government's own interpretation of "neutrality."

The cure for bad speech has always been more speech, not government censorship. That principle applies as much in the digital age as it did when our founders wrote the First Amendment.

PART IV

JOURNALISM'S FREE PRESS CHALLENGES

"It's so important to have a free press, and it is nuts we're not paying more attention to it."

—Jimmy Kimmel, host, *Jimmy Kimmel Live!*

Freedom of the press stands as one of democracy's most essential safeguards, yet it faces challenges today that the founders could scarcely have imagined. Traditional journalism is in crisis—newsrooms are shrinking, trust is eroding, and business models are collapsing under the weight of digital disruption. At the same time, the very definition of "the press" has exploded beyond recognition. Social media influencers command audiences that dwarf legacy newspapers. Citizen journalists break stories from their smartphones. And tech billionaires can silence reporters with the click of a button, then poll their followers about whether to restore their accounts. The question is no longer simply whether we have a free press. Can the protections that have sustained journalism for generations evolve to meet this new reality?

CHAPTER 15

The Risky Game of Crowdsourced Journalism (2022)

———

Last week, Elon Musk raised another public outcry about Twitter's (now X's) operations. It was the latest in a series of dramatic moves he has made since acquiring the social media platform in October. Employees have been leaving in droves, many of them part of a massive layoff that Musk ordered. Users are also migrating to other online platforms, and advertisers are rethinking how much to spend while the chaos continues to unfold.

Musk's latest jaw-dropping moment involved the suspension of seven journalists who were reporting on real-time data about Musk's plane that is publicly available. Musk deemed this to be threatening to his personal safety, even indicating that news about such information might lead to his assassination.

But within hours after the suspension took effect, Musk reversed course by deciding to have the matter resolved by conducting a quick, unscientific survey on Twitter. The results showed that about 59 percent of participating Twitter users who voted favored lifting the suspensions immediately. So Musk proudly reported that "[t]he people have spoken. Accounts who doxxed my location will have their suspension lifted now."

His championing of a public vote on journalistic freedom is not to be lauded, however. It wrongly suggests that there should be some linking of free press values with some type of majority rule. Unfortunately, that line of thinking has been gaining traction nationally.

Exhibit A is "The First Amendment: Where America Stands," a survey by the Freedom Forum conducted in March 2022.[1] This update is the latest in a series that began in 1997, measuring Americans' knowledge and attitudes about our core freedoms: religion, speech, press, assembly, and petition.

More than half (53 percent) of its respondents favor government licensing of journalists. But as Gene Policinski, senior fellow for the First Amendment at the Freedom Forum, noted, "[T]hat's antithetical to either the law or spirit of press freedom—whether such 'permission to collect and report the news' is controlled by the government or a professional group. Our nation's founders had lived through an era of approval of printers by the king—and wanted no part of such a system."

Put simply, freedom of the press, whether as a constitutional mandate or a broader guiding light of our society, should not be decided by a vote. As political commentator and author George Will wisely observed, "[T]here is more to America's purpose, more to justice, than majorities having their way."

Regardless of how seriously one takes Elon Musk's claim that any of these journalists threatened his personal safety through their reporting, there should be a uniform outcry at the notion that their ability to convey such reporting should be decided by the results of a flash poll. And ideally, the best place to voice such disapproval en masse should be on Twitter itself.

CHAPTER 16

The Challenge of Treating Social Media Influencers as Journalists (2024)

The recent announcement by the Democratic National Committee about press credentialing for its nominating convention may have lasting policy implications that are likely to reverberate nationwide.

For the first time, the DNC has determined that social media influencers on platforms such as X, TikTok, and Instagram will be treated on a par with reporters from CNN, major newspapers, and other established media outlets. All will be granted the same press passes to cover the various activities that take place on and off the floor of Chicago's United Center.

Congress has not yet enacted any federal law to establish a reporter's privilege. However, there is pending bipartisan legislation passed unanimously in the House of Representatives and awaiting a vote in the Senate. Given this reality, an open question considering the DNC's action is how much state courts will be willing to protect social media influencers from being compelled to reveal confidential sources before grand juries and other criminal proceedings.

Most states and the District of Columbia grant such protection, either absolutely or conditionally. It is based on a legislative definition of "journalist" to enable someone with a legal justification to refuse to reveal confidential sources under the compulsion of a subpoena.

However, state legislatures have been slow to recognize the dramatic changes in news delivery and audiences in recent years. Given the downsizing of many news and media enterprises and massive layoffs that have left some newsroom staff reduced to bare-bones operations, it should not be surprising that social media influencers have stepped into this void to cover current events firsthand.

The pending federal legislation, the Protect Reporters from Exploitative State Spying (PRESS) Act, can help guide various state legislatures to a common definitional understanding that the DNC has achieved. That bill provides legal protection to those who gather, prepare, collect, photograph, record, write, edit, report or publish news or information "that concerns news events or other matters of public interest for dissemination to the public."

Ideally, these legislatures, and Congress itself in its PRESS Act, will enact laws soon that recognize social media influencers as emerging players in our news and information ecosystem. Their work at the DNC convention will demonstrate that their millions of followers now have additional trusted resources to provide reporting with journalistic integrity.

The question is not whether traditional journalism will survive this disruption—it's whether the legal frameworks that protect press freedom will evolve quickly enough to encompass the new reality of who performs journalistic functions in our democracy.

CHAPTER 17

Let C-SPAN Have Unrestricted Camera Access to US House Proceedings (2023)

After the chaotic process that led to the fifteenth-round election of Rep. Kevin McCarthy (R-CA) as the new Speaker of the House of Representatives, there is much talk about how much power he needed to give up to achieve his narrow-majority victory. But even with the new rule changes for the 118th Congress—such as allowing for a single member to make a motion to vacate, triggering a vote on retaining the Speaker—there is one clear power that Speaker McCarthy has not forfeited. That's the power to let C-SPAN have unrestricted camera access to House proceedings, as it did during the dramatic events leading up to the final vote tally.

What America Saw

American viewers of all political stripes were riveted by seeing, for the first time, how complicated the back-and-forth machinations of our legislators can be. Who will forget the live images of Rep. Mike Rogers (R-AL), the new chairman of the House Armed Services Committee, being forcibly restrained from attacking Rep. Matt Gaetz (R-FL), who refused during the 14th round a vote change to enable Kevin McCarthy to cross the finish line? Or seeing Rep. Marjorie Taylor Greene (R-GA) as she waved around her smartphone with the incoming initials DT to indicate that former president Donald Trump was trying to reach Rep. Matt Rosendale (R-MO) to bring him into the pro-Kevin fold?

The Current Restrictions

Since it began operating on cable television systems nationwide in 1979, C-SPAN has provided live coverage of House sessions. But ever since then, the Speaker has exercised a power provided in that chamber's rules that restricts what the cameras can show to viewers. Given that many legislative activities involve set speeches to only a handful in attendance, viewers are not allowed to see the sparse audience or the reactions of individual members.

It is reality TV in genre, but not in reality itself. The Speaker traditionally has exercised a tight level of audio and visual control that surely will seem anachronistic now that everyone has been able to get a glimpse at the inner workings of a legislative process often described as sausage making.

The Case for More Transparency

Maintaining this new level of transparency seems to have support from Speaker McCarthy's most fervent supporters, too. In his nominating speech for McCarthy on the House floor, Rep. Mike Gallagher (R-WI) succinctly conveyed the larger import of a television policy that would enable voters to see more, even if it lacked the purpose or polish of a congressional press release. "Sure, it looks messy, but democracy is messy. Democracy is messy! Democracy is messy by design. By design! And that's a feature, not a bug of our system. We air it all out in the open for the American people to see because, at the end of the day, the president's not in charge, the Supreme Court's not in charge, and the Speaker of the House is not even in charge; the American people are in charge."

The Opportunity

With the gavel now in Kevin McCarthy's hands, he can make a firm imprint as Speaker by relaxing just when and how widely C-SPAN's cameras can roam. And I suspect that if public opinion is solicited about making such a move, it would overwhelmingly support this new level of civic openness.

Put simply, there is no rational reason to put this proverbial genie back in the bottle. As comedian Jon Stewart noted in a pithy tweet, "This is the best season of C-SPAN ever." The viewers have spoken, and Speaker McCarthy would be well-advised to make sure that our screens remain in living color instead of with a static test pattern once more.

The low visibility of previous congressional proceedings contributed to public disconnection from the legislative process. Now would be the perfect time to embrace transparency as a fundamental democratic value, not just a temporary accident of political chaos.

PART V
LESSONS FROM THE PAST

———

"I'm a big believer in the First Amendment and free speech."
—US Senator John Thune (R-SD),
Republican Majority Leader

Understanding today's challenges requires learning from yesterday's victories. Landmark cases and courageous individuals have expanded the boundaries of permissible expression, often at great personal cost. From a comedian's battle against broadcast censorship to journalists risking jail time to protect press freedom, the fragility and resilience of constitutional protections that we now take for granted deserve continued attention.

CHAPTER 18

George Carlin's American Dream Celebrates the First Amendment (2022)

———

Watching *George Carlin's American Dream*, the Judd Apatow and Michael Bonfiglio two-part HBO Max documentary, was a great time-traveling ride. From the hippy-dippy weatherman on "The Ed Sullivan Show," to hosting the first SNL episode, to playing the genial conductor on "Shining Time Station," the decades flashed before my eyes.

And for me, it brought back memories of my work on a legendary case that the Supreme Court should have refused to hear.

The Seven Dirty Words

That's because there's lots of attention in the documentary devoted to Carlin's hit records, which remain cherished albums in my well-stocked vinyl collection. One notable track was from his stand-up routine—"Seven Words You Can Never Say on Television." These "seven dirty words," according to Carlin, could not be aired by broadcasters regardless of the context or time of day.

And when WBAI-FM, a counter-culture radio station licensed to the Pacifica Foundation, broadcast in full a companion track ("Filthy Words") on Carlin's follow-up album, "Operation Foole" (ironically during a discussion on contemporary language boundaries), his comical assertion of a clear forbidden line was put to the test legally for the first time.

In 1973, John Douglas, an active member of Morality in Media, filed a written complaint with the Federal Communications Commission, stating that his fifteen-year-old son had heard the broadcast on his car radio while they were driving around New York City around 2 p.m. Douglas indicated that this was inappropriate and asked that the FCC investigate the matter.

The Legal Battle

Following Pacifica's investigation and written response, the FCC issued a declaratory order that upheld the Douglas complaint but withheld any penalties against the station. This put WBAI on notice that "in the event subsequent complaints are received, the Commission will then decide whether it should utilize any of the available sanctions it has been granted by Congress."[1]

The cloud that hung over the station due to this "raised eyebrow" of the FCC led Pacifica to appeal the order in federal court. It argued that the FCC's application of an "indecency" standard, which unlike obscenity was not prohibited by law, violated the broadcaster's freedom of speech under the First Amendment. The FCC argued that it had the authority to set content boundaries for what it deemed indecent since it was authorized to grant and renew broadcast licenses by the Communications Act of 1934.

The US Court of Appeals for the District of Columbia Circuit found Pacifica's argument to be persuasive, and in a two to one decision by a three-judge judicial panel, ruled that the FCC had violated the First Amendment by issuing its warning based on "indecent" programming.

My Role in the Case

Unexpectedly, the FCC decided to press on by appealing that decision to the Supreme Court. The Department of Justice, which typically would handle such an appeal, refused to do so since it agreed with the lower court's reasoning. That left the FCC to go it alone.

As a summer law firm associate in Washington, DC between my second and third years at UC Berkeley Law, I found myself suddenly transformed from someone who played the Carlin records over and over to working on the legal brief to convince the Supreme Court not to hear the appeal at all—since the FCC's position could not be squared with established freedom-of-speech precedents under the First Amendment.

The Aftermath

I was part of a losing team since the Supreme Court accepted the FCC's appeal and agreed with it in a five to four ruling, which has given the regulatory agency the power to decide what is indecent in broadcasting ever since then (with some flexibility for late-night programming that Congress later authorized).

In recent years, the Supreme Court has had two cases that allowed it the opportunity to revisit the FCC's authority to punish broadcasters for fleeting expletives and fleeting nudity under the rubric of indecency. But unlike a second federal appeals court, this time in New York, which again found the FCC's actions to violate the First Amendment, the Supreme Court ducked the constitutional issue in favor of a narrower procedural decision that enabled the broadcasters to escape the FCC's wrath in these instances.

Imagine what George Carlin would have to say about that now. The chain of events that he unwittingly unleashed continues to remind us that the American Dream he championed remains one that is still very much worth fighting for.

The Broader Implications

The Carlin case illustrates several enduring principles about free expression in America. First, comedy has always served as a testing ground for free speech boundaries. Comedians often push the envelope precisely because humor can make uncomfortable truths more palatable and challenge social conventions in ways that direct political speech might not.

Second, the case demonstrates how technological change affects constitutional interpretation. When Carlin recorded his routine, radio was a dominant broadcast medium, and the Supreme Court's decision was heavily influenced by broadcasting's "pervasive presence" in American homes. Today, with streaming services, podcasts, and on-demand content, the assumptions underlying the Court's ruling seem increasingly outdated.

Third, the case shows how individual citizens can shape constitutional law. John Douglas's single complaint led to a Supreme Court decision that continues to influence media regulation decades later. His action reminds us that constitutional principles are not abstract legal concepts but living standards that real people invoke when they feel their rights or values are threatened.

The Case's Legacy

The Supreme Court's *Pacifica* decision remains controversial among free speech advocates, who argue that the FCC's authority over broadcast indecency creates a troubling precedent for government content regulation. Critics note that the seven words Carlin highlighted are now commonplace in cable television, streaming services, and even some broadcast programming during late-night hours.

Yet the case also established important boundaries. The Court specifically noted that context matters—the same words that might be problematic during afternoon drive time could be permissible in different circumstances. This contextual approach has influenced how courts and regulators think about speech restrictions more broadly.

What Carlin Would Think Today

George Carlin spent his career challenging authority and questioning social conventions. He understood that language is power, and that controlling language is a way of controlling thought. In his later years, he became increasingly critical of what he saw as the sanitization of American discourse and the growing tendency to avoid difficult conversations about social problems.

If Carlin were alive today, he would likely be fascinated by how his seven words have evolved in the digital age. Some are now routine on cable television and streaming platforms, while others remain taboo in certain contexts. He would probably note the irony that the internet—which allows virtually unlimited access to any kind of content—operates under different rules than the broadcasting system that tried to ban his routine.

More importantly, Carlin would likely see the current debates about campus speech codes, social media content moderation, and "cancel culture" as extensions of the same impulses that led to his case in the first place. His comedy was always about pointing out hypocrisy and challenging people to think more clearly about their assumptions.

The Enduring Lesson

The Carlin case reminds us that free expression rights are not won once and then preserved forever. Each generation must defend these rights in the context of new technologies, social movements, and cultural changes. What seemed like a simple case about seven words on the radio became a landmark decision that continues to influence how we think about the balance between free expression and community standards.

Carlin's real contribution to American free speech was not just his willingness to say forbidden words, but his insistence that language belongs to the people who use it, not to the authorities who would regulate it. His comedy demonstrated that humor can be a powerful tool for social criticism and that laughter can be a form of resistance to excessive authority.

As we face new challenges to free expression in the digital age, Carlin's example reminds us that the fight for free speech often begins with individuals willing to push boundaries, ask uncomfortable questions, and refuse to accept that certain topics are off-limits. The seven words that changed America were really about something much larger: the right of citizens to challenge authority and speak their minds, even when—especially when—their words make others uncomfortable.

The American Dream that Carlin championed wasn't just about the right to pursue happiness, but about the right to define that happiness for yourself, in your own words, on your own terms. That dream, and the constitutional principles that protect it, remain very much worth fighting for always.

CHAPTER 19

Inside the Pentagon Papers Case— a First Amendment Victory Story (2022)

In the 1971 case formally known as *New York Times v. United States*, the Supreme Court weighed whether President Richard Nixon's administration violated the First Amendment by attempting to block the *New York Times* and the *Washington Post* from publishing the Pentagon Papers, a report by Secretary of State Robert McNamara detailing the root causes of the war in Vietnam. Though the court sided with the *Times*, Nixon argued that national security required prior restraint, or government action that preemptively prohibits expression before it occurs.

I spoke in detail with Floyd Abrams, a key member of the legal team for the *Times*, about the behind-the-scenes decision-making involved in the case, and the legal challenges that he was involved in navigating before the Supreme Court.[1]

Floyd Abrams: I became a partner at Cahill Gordon & Reindel in October 1970. Unknown to me, the *New York Times* had been working for a few months on a blockbuster story about the war in Vietnam. Of course, the war there was going terribly. It was getting more and more controversial, as more young men were drafted and more of them were killed in the war.

Secretary of Defense [Robert] McNamara in the late 1960s ordered a study to be prepared about how we got into the war in Vietnam. I've often thought that one would have preferred if the study were made before the war. So the Pentagon Papers were created. That was called the McNamara Report—twenty-three volumes of Defense Department documents, all of them highly classified, and some really secret by their nature.

At that time, there was a consolidated case in the US Supreme Court about confidential sources dealing with three similar cases. I'd worked on the NBC side and in the lower courts, and the media lawyers for the other two cases had an idea. Why don't we do one brief for all of us? The question was who we would get to write such a brief.

We scheduled a meeting to discuss the idea. My suggestion was Alex Bickel, my law professor from Yale. It was clear by then, we thought, that we really had four votes in our favor—the four really liberal guys on the Supreme Court. But we didn't know about anyone else.

Hiring Bickel also would be strategic. He was viewed as a conservative and indeed was a conservative scholar about the Supreme Court— yet one who wrote for *The New Republic* and supported Robert F. Kennedy [in his 1968 presidential bid]. In any event, Bickel was highly respected by the justices on the right of the Court in those days. So Bickel was retained. I was the one that called him to do that. I remember the call very clearly.

Stuart Brotman: Bickel then came for the meeting with the media lawyers in New York, right?

Abrams: Yes, he came in to meet his clients. I don't think he ever had a client. In fact, I know he'd never had a client. There were all these media lawyers in the room. It was June 14, 1971. The Pentagon Papers started to be published on a Sunday. The lunch that I hosted was on a Monday, the next day. So everybody was talking about the *New York Times* and its publication over two days of articles based on this secret study.

Now what I didn't know, and what was unknown outside the *New York Times,* was that the government had threatened the *Times* if they published these articles. There were great internal debates, and this would have involved calls with Attorney General John Mitchell. A telegram was then sent by Mitchell the night of our lunch at which Bickel and I mostly spoke about confidential sources. But we all agreed that the *Times* would be fine.

I've often said that lawyers without clients are the surest people in the world. Why would Nixon go to court? We didn't know. Secretary of State [Henry] Kissinger was telling Nixon about secret negotiations with China, for what later became an important and valuable meeting. Kissinger was saying, "There won't be any respect for the US in China if we can't control our own secrets." The government wrote a telegram to the *New York Times* saying they were going to go to court if the *Times* didn't stop publishing. But Bickel had said at our lunch, "You know, there haven't been prior restraints on journalists publishing the news. And this is the news." Then the telegram arrived at the *Times* threatening litigation if the paper did not stop further publication.

So they called Alex at midnight, one in the morning. They agreed that he needed a law firm to work with.

Brotman: Wasn't this because the law firm representing the *New York Times* declined the case because of a conflict of interest?

Abrams: When the *Times* called their outside law firm that had represented them for sixty years, that firm (headed by former US Attorney General Herbert Brownell)—which had strenuously urged the *Times* not to publish the Pentagon Papers—refused to represent them. So the *Times* found itself without counsel in the most threatening case of its existence, one that their outside counsel had told them could well lead to criminal convictions of the newspaper and its publisher. And that was when, with our luncheon fresh in mind, they called Alex Bickel at midnight and asked him to lead their defense of the case. Bickel had never argued a case in court. But he was a constitutional expert of great distinction and was held in high regard by the Supreme Court, particularly its more conservative members.

With Bickel on board, James Goodale, the *Times'* general counsel, who had strongly urged the newspaper to publish articles based on the Pentagon Papers, called me to ask if I and my firm, Cahill Gordon and Reindel, would work with Bickel in defending the *Times*. I told him that I certainly wanted to do so but would need my firm's approval, which I obtained the next morning.

I picked up Bickel in a taxi about one in the morning from his mother's apartment and the two of us went to my office, where we spent the night first locating and reviewing the Espionage Act, which the government was claiming the *Times* had violated, and then reviewing the most important Supreme Court cases that we thought might be central to the case. The next morning, we received a call from Goodale and proceeded to the *Times* for our first meeting with our client. As we traveled uptown, I wondered if anyone at the *Times* knew that Bickel had never tried any case before and that I, the youngest partner in my firm, had never even been in the Supreme Court before.

Brotman: This must have been before dawn.

Abrams: Absolutely. And we read it for the first time. We went to the *Times* the next morning for a meeting. Neither of us knew anyone on the *Times*, but I knew a good bit by then and started talking about what could happen. The *Washington Post* also was in the picture at that point. During the meeting, a telephone call was received from the lawyer who headed the Civil Division of the US Attorney's Office in New York, saying that the government was going to court at noon. We went to court and appeared before a brand-new judge, Murray Gurfein, just appointed by President Nixon. We went there with Jim Goodale, the general counsel for the *Times*.

It was noteworthy to us that in World War II, Judge Gurfein had been in army intelligence and therefore had had access to classified material. We were sure (and we were right about this) that his military service would be highly relevant, since it could put him more at ease dealing with classified documents and claims of harm from their revelation.

I remember Judge Gurfein saying, "We're all Americans," which we feared (but could not know) was a barb aimed at the *Times* and its lawyers. The government urged him to enter a temporary restraining order. Bickel argued that no such order had ever been entered and that doing so could not be consistent with the First Amendment.

The government was using language about irreparable harm. Judge Gurfein said to us, in effect, "Why don't you give me a chance to study this? So why don't you agree not to publish until a few days later?" Goodale called the *Times*. He was the leader on this. But the answer, which Goodale had urged and we all agreed with, was that for a newspaper, the status quo was the right to print, not enforced silence. The *Times* would continue to publish.

Judge Gurfein then entered the order of prior restraint based on the government's representation of the highly classified nature of the documents and that American POWs were being held. Publishing, the government argued, could interfere with getting them out.

We had a number of meetings at the *Times* during the unusually brief case (it lasted only fifteen days from start to finish) and the one I remember best was at the very beginning of it. It was a meeting chaired by Punch Sulzberger, the *Times* publisher, in which, shortly after the meeting began, he said that whatever the decision of the court was, that the *Times* would obey it.

Tom Wicker, their Washington correspondent and columnist, said, "Punch, I thought that's why we were meeting, to discuss if we were going to obey the order. Let's talk about it." Bickel basically said this to them: "What this is all about, and what we are fighting for in this case, is obedience to law—in this case, the First Amendment. That means abiding by law even if you disagree with it."

I offered a more strategic response, urging on them that if we violated a court order in the case and wound up in the Supreme Court, that the Court would be furious with the *Times*—doing so would make it far more unlikely that we would persuade jurists, who were not fond of the press generally and the *Times* specifically, to rule in our favor.

So everyone at the meeting signed off to obey the order but mount an aggressive legal challenge to it. Thereafter, we had the litigation. Bickel argued just about everything himself. My partner, Bill Hegarty, came to work with him on the secret stuff—national security stuff—which was heard in a secret session of the court.

Brotman: Take me behind the scenes as the litigation began to be organized at your end.

Abrams: From the very beginning of the case, we realized we had one particularly high hurdle to overcome. The nation was at war, American soldiers were dying, with others held as prisoners of war, and the executive branch was representing to the Court that further publication of the Pentagon Papers would do irreparable harm to the nation. In that context, why should the Court intervene? I kept thinking as the case progressed that if we were in the midst of World War II, and a similar issue had arisen that while a court might have ruled for us, it would not have wanted to do so and might well not have done so.

One way to address those fears was to try to persuade the Supreme Court that the government was exaggerating the potential for harm from the *Times*' publication. Accordingly, we obtained affidavits from high-ranking former State Department and CIA officials stating that publication of the sort of material in the Pentagon Papers was not really harmful to the war effort, that what they revealed was not weapons technology, plans of military operations, or the like. We were helped, we thought, by the reality that what the Pentagon Papers themselves demonstrated was a pattern of government falsehoods through the years about the Vietnam conflict, a pattern that we did not quite say, but inevitably inferred, was continuing into the case.

The cross-examination by my partner, Bill Hegarty, of a chief military witness for the government was extremely helpful in this respect, since it showed that the witness was upset about even the least revealing information about national defense. At the same time, we sought to minimize any supposed harm from publication of the Pentagon Papers by the submission of a superb affidavit by Max Frankel, former executive editor of *the Times*, about well-established norms in Washington. Even classified information was commonly made available to journalists by government officials for a variety of motivations—personal and policy-related—which had the impact of significantly informing the public. The publication of portions of the Pentagon Papers, Frankel argued, was one example of that.

There were a number of hearings in the case, including a particularly threatening one that I argued. That was the government directing the *Times* to turn over the Pentagon Papers that they had, which we were immediately told would compromise the identity of the source because his fingerprints were all over it. At that point, Daniel Ellsberg was not visible and not known. His name was unknown to us, too. But we were told that the source could be discovered, so I argued on that issue.

At that time, the *Times* had another case in the courts in California on the issue of confidential sources. One of their journalists, Earl Caldwell, had been subpoenaed and was protected by a court order that was on appeal. That was one of the cases that went to the Supreme Court later, the case I mentioned that Bickel had been called in to write a combined brief for media companies.

So my argument was not to make us have to turn over the documents. Bickel came up with the idea: "Well, why can't you tell them what documents you have, without actually giving them?" Which we did and which they promptly forgot. But it turned out to be really important. The *Times* would not have complied with that order; they would not have turned over the actual Pentagon Papers that they had, thinking that it would compromise the source. If that happened, then everything would have gotten off the tracks. The Supreme Court was not about to protect journalists who were violating court orders to judges. We would have a real problem if the case went to the Supreme Court.

Brotman: And you knew the Pentagon Papers case would be going to go to Supreme Court.

Abrams: We knew. But it was very fortuitous that we told the judges about what was in the documents without actually turning them over.

Brotman: It sounds like you all were on a twenty-four-seven schedule.

Abrams: We were all working day and night. No one's sleeping, and no one knows anything anymore. You forget things. I don't mean now. I mean then.

Brotman: You had a relatively small legal team, right?

Abrams: Well, we had like eight people. But in terms of who knows this or that, it was very small. The government continued to maintain, throughout the case, that the *Times* had certain documents that were not on our list. But it's not because they thought we lied; they paid no attention to the list we gave them.

Brotman: And in lightning speed, the case reaches the Supreme Court.

Abrams: It took fifteen days, from beginning to end. Bickel's argument in the Supreme Court had one central moment. He thought, and I thought, that was when he was answering the question of Justice Potter Stewart, who asked in effect, "Suppose when we go back to our chambers and we read the Pentagon Papers, we find that publication of material at issue would result in the death of twenty American young men who simply had the misfortune to have a low number in terms of being drafted. Is your position then that we must allow you to publish?"

Bickel started, and lawyers often do this, with, "That's not this case." That was true, but it also was an answer that frequently irritates judges who know that and are posing hypothetical questions to explore the breadth of an argument. Finally, Bickel said that if this were the situation, then his dedication to the First Amendment would clash with his dedication to the security of the country. And yes, the *Times* would not publish that. That answer was viewed as such a sellout by the ACLU that they submitted a brief denouncing it. I thought they were wrong, terribly wrong, and that his answer was absolutely required for an advocate for the *Times* to make.

Brotman: Were you aware they were going to file that?

Abrams: Not in advance. The case came and went, it was over on June 30. We won six to three. I have been struck by the fact that even the justices who voted for us had been persuaded by the government that publication would do some harm. They were wrong about that. But basically they said the government had failed to prove that the amount of harm that would be done outweighed the First Amendment, so the near-total ban on prior restraints carried the day and we prevailed.

Brotman: How important was it that the *Times* was the client?

Abrams: It was very important that the *Times* was the client during the case. A less respected entity might well have lost the case. But even as to the *Times*, there remained the risk, as indicated by what some of the justices observed, that there could still be an Espionage Act prosecution of the *Times* after publication. In effect, the Supreme Court suggested if the *Times* wanted to take the chance that it was going to be indicted, you know, this remained a risk at that point.

Brotman: What advice were you providing about this potential criminal prosecution?

Abrams: We didn't really have a strong view as to what would have happened regarding a charge of breaching the Espionage Act. We had argued to Justice [Thurgood] Marshall, who agreed with us on this, that the Espionage Act didn't cover journalists reporting news in good faith. Marshall went along with that, but certainly Justice [Byron] White and Justice Stewart did not. That did not happen, though. So the case really was over.

The Lasting Impact

The Pentagon Papers case established several crucial precedents that continue to protect press freedom today. Most importantly, it set an extremely high bar for prior restraint—the government's ability to stop publication before it occurs. The Court's decision made clear that the government must meet an almost impossible standard to justify preventing publication, even when national security is claimed to be at stake.

The case also demonstrated the vital role that sources play in democratic accountability. Daniel Ellsberg, who leaked the Pentagon Papers, understood that the American people had a right to know how their government had made decisions about Vietnam. His willingness to risk criminal prosecution—he was later indicted under the Espionage Act, though charges were eventually dropped—illustrates the courage required to challenge government secrecy.

Furthermore, the case showed how institutional support for press freedom can make the difference between victory and defeat. The *Times'* willingness to risk its business, its broadcast licenses, and its executives' freedom sent a powerful message about the importance of independent journalism. The newspaper's decision to continue publishing despite a court order demonstrates the kind of institutional courage that democracy requires.

Lessons for Today

The Pentagon Papers case offers several lessons for contemporary debates about press freedom and government secrecy. First, it reminds us that prior restraint remains the most dangerous threat to press freedom. While the government can prosecute journalists after publication (though this is rare and controversial), the ability to stop publication entirely would fundamentally alter the relationship between press and government.

Second, the case illustrates the importance of having legal frameworks that protect whistleblowers and sources. The Pentagon Papers could not have been published without Ellsberg's willingness to leak classified documents. Contemporary debates about the Espionage Act and whistleblower protections echo the same tensions that animated the Pentagon Papers case.

Third, the case demonstrates that press freedom depends not just on constitutional protections, but on institutional courage by news organizations. The *Times'* decision to publish despite enormous pressure shows the kind of independence that effective journalism requires. In an era when news organizations face economic pressures and political attacks, the Pentagon Papers case reminds us what is at stake when press freedom is threatened.

Finally, the case illustrates the complex relationship between national security and democratic transparency. The government's claims about potential harm from publication proved largely unfounded, but the case established procedures for courts to review such claims *in camera* when necessary. This balance between secrecy and transparency remains one of the most challenging issues in democratic governance.

The Pentagon Papers' Enduring Legacy

Fifty years later, the Pentagon Papers case remains one of the Supreme Court's most important decisions protecting press freedom. It established the principle that the press serves as a check on government power, even—especially—when that government claims to be protecting national security. The case showed that democracy depends on citizens having access to information about their government's actions, even when those actions are controversial or embarrassing.

The courage shown by the *New York Times*, its lawyers, and Daniel Ellsberg continues to inspire journalists and citizens who believe that democratic accountability requires transparency about government actions. In an era when press freedom faces new challenges from both government officials and private actors, the Pentagon Papers case reminds us that protecting the right to publish is essential to protecting democracy itself.

As Floyd Abrams reflected years later, the Pentagon Papers case was about more than just one newspaper's right to publish classified documents. It was about whether American democracy would allow its citizens to know the truth about their government's actions, even when that truth is uncomfortable or inconvenient for those in power. The Supreme Court's decision to protect that right remains one of the most important victories for press freedom in American history.

CHAPTER 20

Let's Not Create a Self-Censorship Wave in Comedy (2025)

"I definitely don't think that the government should be involved, ever, in dictating what a comedian can or cannot say in a monologue."

—Joe Rogan, host, *The Joe Rogan Experience*

Stephen Colbert's recent announcement that he has been terminated from hosting *The Late Show* on CBS has been met with confusion and anger by millions of his fans. The network's press announcement indicated that the cancellation, effective in May 2026, was the result solely of financial losses for the top-rated series.

However, a larger concern remains that a contributing factor was the punishment of Colbert's sharp political jokes, which frequently targeted the Trump administration, versions one and two. Removing both Colbert and eliminating *The Late Show* after he departs may have a more lasting impact on other comedians now on air or in the future.

The Legacy of Lenny Bruce

Sixty-two years ago, there was a famous edgy comedian who was assaulted onstage in Los Angeles. Lenny Bruce was placed in handcuffs, thrown into a police van, and arraigned at the precinct station with fingerprints and a mug shot. Bruce was charged with violating California's obscenity law and would continue to be arrested there on the same charges that year and in 1964.

Although not convicted in these incidents, Bruce realized that the harassment would not end, so he took his act, which included bits such as "Infidelity," "Guys are Carnal," and "To Come is a Preposition" to New York City. But he had no better luck there. Undercover investigators from the NYPD were waiting for him to perform at the Café Au Go Go in Greenwich Village, and he was hauled off for violating New York Penal Code 1104, which barred "obscene, indecent, immoral and impure drama, play, exhibition, and entertainment . . . which would lead to the corruption of the morals of youth and others."

After a grand jury indictment, Bruce was brought to trial and convicted. The court found his jokes "appealed to prurient interest," were "patently offensive to the average person in the community," and lacked "redeeming social value." He was sentenced to four months of incarceration in a workhouse, a penalty that remained on the books even after he died of a morphine overdose before the case reached a New York appellate court.

It was not until 2003 that Gov. George Pataki issued Lenny Bruce a posthumous pardon—the first one ever in the state's history. Pataki characterized it as "a declaration of New York's commitment to upholding the First Amendment."

The Chilling Effect of Self-Censorship

That brings us to what Colbert's CBS termination may produce—a new wave of self-censorship among comedians who find it to be the most practical route to avoid a pink slip. They will not need to have a formal explanation that they have been removed because, in the eyes of some, their jokes lacked "redeeming social value." It will be easier to tone things down to leave the klieg lights burning.

Is this the shape of things to come? Instinctively, regardless of political leanings, we all know that a world without the sharp edges of comedy is not the world we want to live in.

PART VI

BROADCASTING AND THE CONSTITUTION

"I think it is unbelievably dangerous for the government to put itself in the position of saying we're going to decide what speech we like and what we don't, and we're going to threaten to take you off air if we don't like what you're saying."

—US Senator Ted Cruz (R-TX)

Broadcasting occupies an unusual place in American constitutional law—being simultaneously protected by the First Amendment and subject to government oversight that would be unthinkable for newspapers or books. For nearly a century, this paradox has rested on a dominant justification: the electromagnetic spectrum is a scarce public resource that cannot accommodate every voice, so those granted licenses to use it must serve as trustees for "the public interest."

As technology erodes the scarcity rationale that justified broadcast regulation in the first place, we must ask whether the public trustee model still serves democracy—or whether it has become an invitation for government interference in editorial decisions that the First Amendment was designed to protect.

CHAPTER 21

Airwaves Regulation and the First Amendment (2025)

Under the First Amendment of the Constitution, freedom of speech and freedom of the press are fundamental rights. This underscores our national commitment, both in law and in spirit, to ensuring that citizens receive the widest possible diversity of ideas and information. Our unique and powerful dedication to these principles aims at preserving and enhancing "an uninhibited marketplace of ideas in which truth will ultimately prevail."

This is the fundamental principle of the First Amendment, upon which, in the words of distinguished jurist Learned Hand, "we have staked our all."

The First Amendment is directly related to our electoral system and constitutional form of government. By maximizing media outlets and individual voices, we increase the possibility of more diverse information reaching the public; this, in turn, helps them participate better as voters and citizens in an increasingly complex social order.

The Paradox of Government Regulation

Government regulation in the United States, particularly regulation of electronic mass media, historically has played an important role in furthering our First Amendment principle of diversified control of media outlets. However, regulation also has created situations that are antithetical to the First Amendment—namely, an increasingly intrusive role that the Federal Communications Commission (FCC), a government agency delegated by Congress to regulate radio and television in the public interest, has played in overseeing program content.

Broadcast regulation in the United States stems from two competing goals of the First Amendment: maximizing media diversity and preserving a free press where editors, rather than government representatives, make the ultimate decisions concerning information that the public will receive.

Mass media in the United States, including newspapers, radio, and television, have developed within the framework of a free enterprise system. They have been funded by private capital—individuals and stockholders of corporations—and have been supported largely by revenues derived from advertisers who utilize them to sell their products and services to consumers.

The Benefits of Competition

Private sector development of mass communications has yielded an important benefit—innovation spurred by competition. This has been particularly true in electronic media, specifically radio, where most urban centers now have a multiplicity of stations.

The result of free market competition is that these radio stations develop specialized audiences. Competition has yielded several innovative programming formats, including all-news, call-in talk programs, and classical music stations. This development of a variety of media outlets and formats is fully consistent with the First Amendment goal of diversity.

The Problem of Concentration

Private sector development of mass media, however, also has created a negative effect that undermines the First Amendment. Increasingly, large corporations have become owners of multiple broadcast properties in major cities; they have also become cross-media owners, so that a number now own newspapers and radio or television stations in the same area.

Although there are just a handful of cases where a true media monopoly exists, where the only newspaper and radio and television station is commonly owned, the trend toward increased concentration of media outlets is very apparent. While empirical studies have produced no definitive answer as to how the concentration of control ultimately influences the flow of information in a community, the aggregation of control, by itself, is enough of a threat to our First Amendment goal of maximum diversity to involve the government and its powers of regulation.

Two Approaches to Regulation

Government regulation aimed at controlling the power of private media entities has taken two main routes:

Structural regulation seeks to maximize diversity by limiting the number and combination of media outlets that can be owned by a single individual or corporate entity.

Behavioral regulation looks at individual cases to see if the media outlet is impeding the reception of a diverse range of views.

The federal government has also varied the intrusiveness of regulation in general by distinguishing print media from electronic media.

Why Broadcasting Gets Different Treatment

There are several explanations for this distinction. Broadcasting undoubtedly has a unique impact upon the American people: radio is everywhere—in the car, in the home, and in the street; television has an even greater impact because, on average, a television set is turned on in an American household for about six hours a day.

The Supreme Court itself has acknowledged this rationale of "uniquely pervasive presence" as a legal basis for having the government regulate "indecent" programming that would in any other situation be characterized as protected speech under the First Amendment. There are serious shortcomings, however, with this line of reasoning. If broadcast radio and television have too much power, it does not follow that the answer should undermine important constitutional protections. Rather, where appropriate, antitrust or similar trade regulation laws should be used to directly limit media concentration.

The Spectrum Scarcity Argument

The best explanation for the unique treatment of broadcasting under the First Amendment stems from spectrum scarcity. Broadcast radio and television, which utilize the electromagnetic spectrum, are inherently not open to all, so that government licensing of broadcast stations is necessary to prevent chaotic interference.

Licensing distinguishes broadcasting from print media, but it is simplistic to base the present regulatory structure solely on the necessity of licensing. The government could have auctioned the frequency to the highest bidder, or given leases with "rent" payments, or used a common carrier-type approach, where access would be assured to many. Congress decided, however, to give short-term licenses solely on the condition that the recipient volunteers to serve the public interest.

The Public Trustee Model

The public trustee scheme is the second reason for distinguishing broadcasting from print media. It can be argued that, considering government licensing, some form of access to ventilate issues of public importance is necessary. But this does not necessarily mandate that there be a regulatory scheme that requires the broadcaster to act as a public trustee. Rather, as a matter of both sound policy and constitutional principle, the government should select the approach that accomplishes this purpose with the least interference with the First Amendment right of editorial discretion.

Congress, however, never approached the issue on these terms. It did not want censorship, but at the same time, it sought to impose the notion that a broadcast license embodied a public trust, although it did not really know what the regulatory structure would be. The FCC, rather unfairly, was thrust into the role of "overseer" and "ultimate arbiter and guardian" of the public interest, even though no objective meaning was attached to that phrase.

Chief Justice Warren Burger, in *Columbia Broadcasting System, Inc. v. Democratic National Committee*, quite correctly acknowledged that these regulatory tasks call for "a delicate balancing of competing interests," and that the "maintenance of this balance for more than eighty years has called on both the regulators and the licensees to walk a 'tightrope' to preserve the First Amendment values written into the Communications Act."[1]

Moving Toward a Marketplace Model

In regulating broadcasting, the FCC has emphasized the behavioral model too much; it is engaging in ad hoc oversight of programming decisions. This is in sharp contrast to the content-neutral approach that the government applies to the print media. Yet from a First Amendment point of view, and in terms of our national well-being, this print regulatory model has worked very well. One need only look at the great diversity in books and magazines, and the absence of any government content control, other than obscenity or copyright, to see that media diversity can be promoted through minimal behavioral regulation.

Ultimately, the best way for the government to promote diversity and competition among media voices is to move toward a marketplace model. New opportunities to utilize the existing broadcast spectrum more efficiently, so that additional competitive outlets are possible, should be pursued vigorously. Additionally, private sector development of new communications technologies should continue without burdensome and unnecessary governmental regulation.

Government should intervene only to ensure fair effective competition (e.g., enforcing antitrust laws) and where the marketplace is skewed and cannot be corrected by competitive forces. Technology will alleviate many, if not all, of the problems of scarcity that presently exist, which in turn are used to justify a lesser form of First Amendment protection for broadcasters.

But technological development is a dynamic evolutionary process, and we must deal with the reality of what to do in the interim. We should now reassess how the behavioral approach to regulation has eroded our First Amendment interest in a free press, and how content-neutral approaches would strengthen this interest.

CHAPTER 22

Revisiting the Broadcast Public Interest Standard in Communications Law and Regulation (2017)

In a January 2017 interview with the trade publication *Variety*, former Federal Communications Commission Chairman Tom Wheeler made a revealing comment less than a week before he stepped down:

"My 'aha' moment was that the public interest was a pretty malleable concept. The public interest is determined by the adage, 'Where you stand depends on where you sit.' And so, what I have tried to do is say, 'OK, we need another standard.' And I kept saying to myself, 'What is it that is in the common good, as differentiated from the public interest?' Because the common good is how you can serve the good of the most people the best way."[1]

Wheeler's remark underscored an existential question in communications law and regulation: What does the mandate to regulate broadcasting consistent with the "public interest, convenience, and necessity" really mean?

The presence of this powerful legal, regulatory, and philosophical phrase in the Communications Act of 1934 is clear. Yet the legislative, judicial, and regulatory history of its interpretation reflects decades of uncertainty and ambiguity by Congress, reviewing courts, and the FCC itself.

Legislative History: A Standard Without Definition

Under the 1912 Radio Act, it was illegal to transmit on the radio without a license from the Department of Commerce, which actively policed broadcast stations to minimize technical interference. A successful 1926 challenge ended this regulatory scheme, and interference problems escalated everywhere. A new allocation method had to be found.

Free speech advocates from religious, educational, and labor groups argued that a common carrier approach would be best by requiring broadcasters to allow anyone to buy airtime. The commercial broadcasters, represented by the National Association of Broadcasters (NAB), opposed common carrier status, seeking to retain editorial control over programming and to merge individual stations into national networks.

Congress adopted a compromise between the industry and the free speech advocates. With the Radio Act of 1927, and later the Communications Act of 1934 (which has been amended periodically and remains the charter for broadcast radio and television today), two core principles were established:

First, Congress prohibited common carriage for broadcasters and mandated a government-controlled, short-term licensing regime that assigned broadcasters to designated channels in the electromagnetic spectrum.

Second, to justify this exclusionary zoning policy, Congress also required that broadcasters act as trustees of spectrum on behalf of all the others who were kept off the airwaves by the government. As guardians of a scarce and publicly owned resource, broadcasters were required to operate in the "public interest, convenience and necessity."

The Problem of Undefined Terms

However, Congress failed to define what it meant by "public interest" in either the statutory text or the legislative history, leading one commentator to posit that the phrase meant "as little as any phrase that the drafters of the Act could have used and still comply with the constitutional requirement that there be some standard to guide the administrative wisdom of the licensing authority."[2]

Because Congress had delegated to the Federal Radio Commission (FRC) the power to determine virtually all aspects of broadcasting, the FRC became the sole arbiter of what constituted the "public interest."

Yet in its short seven-year existence, the FRC never issued a coherent definition of the public interest standard. Instead, it made case-by-case determinations of individual station practices that satisfied the standard.

The legislative history of the 1927 Act also does not explain the origins of the broadcast public interest standard. One explanation of this absence is that when the drafters of the Radio Act reached an impasse in their attempt to define a standard, a young lawyer on loan to the Senate from the Interstate Commerce Commission suggested the words "public interest, convenience and necessity"—the standard used in the Interstate Commerce Act. The drafters agreed.

The Communications Act of 1934 incorporated virtually all the 1927 Act's regulatory structure as it pertained to broadcasting. The "public interest, convenience, and necessity" phrase once again received no definition. Instead, the 1934 Act delegated implicit authority to the FCC to interpret these obligations.

Judicial Attempts at Clarification

Beginning with the 1927 Radio Act and continuing with the 1934 Communications Act, several key judicial decisions have addressed the implementation of the broadcast public interest standard. Here are some highlights:

KFKB Broadcasting Ass'n v. Federal Radio Commission (1931): The first significant federal court case to address the meaning of regulating in the "public interest." The D.C. Circuit held that the FRC's refusal to renew a license based on the content of that station's past programming did not constitute censorship.

Trinity Methodist Church v. Federal Radio Commission (1932): Here, the FRC again relied on the public interest standard of the 1927 Act to deny a license renewal to a radio station based on the content of its programming. The same court affirmed the FRC's finding that radio station KGEF's broadcasts were not in the public interest because they "obstructed the administration of justice, offended the religious suscep-tibilities of thousands, inspired political distrust and civic discord . . . and offended youth and innocence by the free use of words suggestive of sexual immorality."

Federal Radio Commission v. Nelson Bros. Bond & Mortgage Co. (1933): The US Supreme Court held that the public interest standard's lack of definition does not grant the Federal Radio Commission unlimited power. Rather, the Commission was limited to consider the advan-tages enjoyed by the people of the state and their reasonable demands and the services rendered by respective stations, among other factors.

Federal Communications Commission v. Pottsville Broadcasting (1940): The US Supreme Court in this case upheld the public interest stan-dard, calling it the "touchstone" of authority of the FCC and holding that the Commission's responsibility always was to measure applica-tions via this standard. According to this opinion, the public inter-est standard is "as concrete as the complicated factors for judgment in such a field of delegated authority permit" and the approach is "a supple instrument for the exercise of discretion."

Federal Communications Commission v. Sanders Bros. Radio Station (1940): Here, the US Supreme Court held that the public interest stan-dard did not require the FCC to consider economic injury to existing broadcast stations when considering an application for a new station. But unlike the Pottsville Broadcasting case, the Court offered a nar-rower interpretation of the public interest standard, suggesting the FCC had no supervisory control over programs, business matters, or station policies.

National Broadcasting Co. v. United States (1943): The US Supreme Court found the analogy between broadcast media and print appro-priate and focused particularly on the nature of the medium. As the broadcast spectrum was not free to all, but rather was held for the public trust, there existed a parallel duty to maintain a broadcast media in the "public interest." Consequently, the Court held that the 1934 Communications Act confers broad power upon the FCC to regulate broadcasters in the public interest. It defined the public interest as the interest of the listening public in "the larger and more effective use of radio." Radio frequencies, unlike other modes of communication, are limited and therefore not available to all; this is what subjects it to government regulation. The Court also rejected the argument that the public interest standard is sufficiently vague to represent an unconstitutional delegation of power.

WOKO, Inc. v. Federal Communications Commission (1946): The US Supreme Court, in finding no abuse of discretion by the FCC, held that it was up to the Commission, rather than the courts, to be satisfied that the granting of a broadcast license renewal would be in the public interest, thereby reversing the holding of the US Court of Appeals for the DC Circuit.

Federal Communications Commission v. RCA Communications, Inc. (1953): The US Supreme Court held that competition alone does not necessarily further the public convenience, interest, or necessity. Competition may be considered as a factor in public interest policymaking as long as competition or its absence is not the single overriding principle directing the FCC's activity.

McClatchy Broadcasting v. Federal Communications Commission (1956): The federal appellate court in the D.C. Circuit held that the public interest standard does not lend itself to a "precise or comprehensive definition." However, the only restrictions the court would place on the Commission were that it must act neither arbitrarily nor capriciously and that it must act within statutory and constitutional bounds. This holding has been criticized as obvious and not particularly illuminating.

Red Lion Broadcasting Co. v. Federal Communications Commission (1970): The US Supreme Court, for the first time focusing on the First Amendment rights of broadcasters, unanimously upheld the constitutionality of the "Fairness Doctrine," which required broadcasters to present both sides of controversial issues that were the subject of their broadcasts.

Unlike in print media, radio and television broadcasting spectrum limits the number of voices that can be heard at any given time and therefore gives the government the ability to set content requirements to maximize the public benefits derived from broadcasting. Therefore, the Court held the Commission could regulate licenses to assure stations served the public interest.

Columbia Broadcasting System, Inc. v. Democratic Nat. Committee (1973): The US Supreme Court found that determining the best interest of the public is difficult and that deference must be given to Congress and the experience of the FCC, while remaining sensitive to First Amendment interests. It held that "Congress intended to permit private broadcasting to develop with the widest journalistic freedom consistent with its public obligations. Only when the interests of the public are found to outweigh the private journalistic interests of the broadcasters will government power be asserted within the framework of the 1934 Act. License renewal proceedings, in which the listening public can be heard, are a principal means of such regulation."

The FCC's Evolving Approach

Internally, the FCC has been active in assessing the importance of the statutory public interest standard for broadcasting. Former FCC Commissioner Ervin Dugan observed that "successive regimes at the FCC have oscillated wildly between enthusiasm for the public interest standard and distaste for it." FCC Chairman Newton Minow, appointed by President Kennedy, has written that the words "public interest" are "at the heart of what Congress did in 1934, and they remain at the heart of our tomorrows."[3]

"Whatever the temptations to abandon this notion—and they are many—the stakes are too high," Minow observed. "Without commitment to the public interest, all government action vis-à-vis communications would be without meaning."[4]

The FCC has said that "our general mandate . . . calls for consideration of other factors and a balancing of all relevant factors by this Commission in assessing the public interest." It has further clarified that the statutory duty to broadcast in the "public interest" imposed on licensees the obligation to be sensitive to problems of public concern in the community and to make sufficient time available for a full discussion of such problems on a non-discriminatory basis.

The FCC has also interpreted the Communications Act's public interest guideline as requiring diversity of ownership to maximize diversity of viewpoints.

The Commission has stated that Congress deliberately placed the public interest standard in the Communications Act to provide the Commission with maximum flexibility in dealing with the ever-changing conditions of the field of broadcasting:

"The Commission was not created solely to provide certainty. Rather, Congress established a mandate for the Commission to act in the public interest. We conceive of that interest to require us to regulate where necessary, to deregulate where warranted, and above all, to assure the maximum service to the public at the lowest cost and with the least amount of regulation and paperwork."[5]

Taken together, both the courts and the FCC have noted that the words "public interest" imply a balancing of all relevant factors that the agency is to consider. Courts review the Commission's decisions to determine whether the FCC has fairly exercised its discretion within the vague bounds expressed by the public interest standard. In reviewing public interest determinations, appellate courts are faced with a three-part inquiry:

1. Is a particular factor under consideration by the FCC legally relevant? "An agency's determination that a certain factor is a relevant consideration in the public interest balancing test is, in essence, an interpretation of the agency's enabling act regarding the scope of the agency's authority. Although courts have shown some deference to an agency's interpretation of its own statute, the standard of review of this question of law should be stricter than that used to review questions of fact or the agency's reasoning process."[6]

2. How should questions of fact be resolved? "For example, once the FCC determines that the efficiency of a communications service is a relevant factor, it must next determine whether the proposed service for which a license is sought is truly more efficient than existing ones."[7]

3. How should the FCC's decision-making process, or the actual balancing of proper considerations, be reviewed?" This is essentially a review of the agency's reasoning process. Courts normally apply an 'arbitrary and capricious' standard at this stage, overturning only agency determinations that amount to abuses of discretion."[8]

The Communications Act of 1934 also provides more specific guidelines for close cases. For example, if more than one applicant requests the same broadcast channel, then the FCC must determine which applicant will best serve the public interest. And if the applicants are equally qualified, the Commission must select randomly among them to award the license.

Overall, regarding broadcast license renewals, applications historically have been granted with few exceptions. In recent years, with the implementation of the postcard renewal application, the FCC has truncated its evaluation by requesting a minimal amount of information regarding a broadcast licensee's satisfaction of license renewal criteria under the public interest standard.

The FCC lacks the power to remove the basic statutory framework of the public interest standard; however, the more autonomy the Commission grants to its licensees, the more its interpretation of the public trusteeship model has come to resemble primarily a marketplace approach. Although some commentators have argued that the FCC is abandoning the statutory public interest approach in favor of the marketplace, the FCC disagrees by arguing that the public interest can be met through reliance on market forces.

Because the 1934 Act embraced a public trusteeship model instead of a pure marketplace one, courts have maintained limits on the extent that the FCC can utilize market mechanisms as a spectrum allocation alternative. If the Commission were to go so far as to remove all restrictions on a licensee's use of spectrum, the regulation of spectrum in the public interest would begin to resemble a granting of statutorily prohibited property interests.

The FCC has not moved beyond these judicial limits to date. None of its recent deregulatory initiatives has granted broadcast licensees the autonomy to change the principal use of Commission-allocated spectrum from broadcasting to some other type of telecommunications service that may be justified by market forces rather than by a more generalized public interest standard.

Contemporary Critiques and Alternatives

Three critiques of the public interest standard are worthy of review:

Former National Telecommunications and Information Administration Administrator Henry Geller suggests an alternative system that he believes will work more successfully: "The basic goal of the FCC is to improve the quality and educational aspects of broadcast programs. That goal, however, is not being achieved. The self-interest of the broadcaster and the whole economic structure of the commercial broadcasting industry work against the notion of the broadcaster as public fiduciary. [9]

For example, children watch a great deal of television, over thirty hours a week. One would expect that the role of a public trustee would include broadcasting programs with educational content, such as *Sesame Street*. The broadcasting industry has the money and the resources to do it, but it does not."

Geller favors eliminating the current system of a public interest standard applied to broadcasting. He would replace it with a system that collects a percentage of gross revenues of a broadcast station under a long-term contract and use that money to accomplish the public interest goals of informational children's programming. The benefit of this plan "would provide a more direct solution to the problem of finding quality, noncommercial programming."

Peter Huber, senior fellow at the Manhattan Institute, contends that the FCC and the courts have failed to build up a body of precedent that would imbue the public interest standard with any concrete, durable meaning: "The 'public interest' is, to put it mildly, an amorphous standard that allows the Commission to consider virtually anything. As the Supreme Court has said, the 'standard no doubt leaves wide discretion and calls for imaginative interpretation.' It is 'not a standard that lends itself to application with exactitude.' . . . Congress is similarly hindered in trying to evaluate the agency's policy when it is implemented in this fashion; thus, Congress cannot exercise effective oversight."[10]

In contrast, Randolph May, president of The Free State Foundation, argues that Congress should revise the Communications Act to set forth more specific guidance for the FCC. In today's environment of digital convergence in which competition is flourishing across communications sectors, May asserts that Congress should not wait to be compelled by the courts to replace the public interest standard with more specific guidance to the FCC. May hopes this guidance will provide an unmistakable roadmap toward a deregulatory system consistent with a competitive marketplace:

> "Strictly speaking, the public interest standard may have been no less constitutionally suspect at the time of its inclusion in the original 1934 Act than today. . . . The standard sure turned out to be the 'supple instrument' in the hands of the agency that [Justice] Frankfurter envisioned. Now, though, Congress must ask itself anew whether the public interest standard is sufficiently 'concrete' to fulfill Congress's responsibility to set communications policies for the Information Age, or whether it is so vague that it can mean whatever three FCC Commissioners say it means on any given day."[11]

The Digital Television Advisory Committee's Recommendations

President Clinton established the Advisory Committee on the Public Interest Obligations of Digital Television Broadcasters in March 1997. The goal of the Committee was to determine how the principles of public trusteeship that had governed broadcast television should be applied in the wake of the Telecommunications Act of 1996, which amended but did not replace the Communications Act of 1934. Specifically, the President requested that the Advisory Committee advise on the public interest obligations of digital television broadcasters, which would replace analog broadcasting techniques as the new transmission technology.

The recommendations of the Advisory Committee represent one of the most sustained and thorough inquiries into the public interest obligations of television broadcasters ever conducted. For example:

1. Digital broadcasters should be required to make enhanced disclosures of their public interest programming and activities on a quarterly basis, using standardized check-off forms that reduce administrative burdens and can be easily understood by the public.

2. The National Association of Broadcasters, acting as the representative of the broadcasting industry, should draft an updated voluntary Code of Conduct to highlight and reinforce the public interest commitments of broadcasters.

3. The FCC should adopt a set of minimum public interest requirements for digital television broadcasters.

4. Congress should create a trust fund to ensure enhanced and permanent funding for public broadcasting to help it fulfill its potential in the digital television environment and remove it from the vicissitudes of the political process.

5. The television broadcast industry should voluntarily provide five minutes each night for candidate-centered discourse in the thirty days before an election. Blanket bans on the sale of airtime to all state and local political candidates also should be examined.

6. Broadcasters should work with appropriate emergency communications specialists and manufacturers to determine the most effective means to transmit disaster warning information. The means chosen should be minimally intrusive on bandwidth and not result in undue additional burdens or costs on broadcasters.

7. Diversity is an important value in broadcasting, whether it is in programming, political discourse, hiring, promotion, or business opportunities within the industry. The Advisory Committee recommended that broadcasters seize the opportunities inherent in digital television technology to substantially enhance the diversity available in the television marketplace.

Despite these recommendations and the numerous changes that the 1996 Act introduced, the FCC's vague mandate to act in the "public interest" remained. The 1996 Act clarified that the standard is applicable to television in the digital era, however, which only maintained the legislative status quo. It does not provide any guidance for or limitations on the kinds of rules and regulations the FCC can adopt in articulating its presumptive understanding of the public interest or its regulatory role. In the intervening years, this absence of a statutory definition remains, and only Congress can remedy this continuing lack of legislative boundaries that it has provided to the FCC.

Looking Forward

The FCC's mandate to regulate broadcasting consistent with the "public interest, convenience, and necessity" remains a pillar of communications law and regulation. Its legacy from the early part of the twentieth century endures, yet its precise meaning remains opaque and elusive.

The decades-long lack of clarity calls for more focused legislative attention to what decisional guidance should be delegated to the FCC. Absent any Congressional action, the FCC can and should articulate a set of public interest principles that can be applied to broadcasting with greater transparency and consistency.

CHAPTER 23

Will the FCC's "Public Interest" Standard Limit Broadcast Free Speech? (2025)

"I do not want the FCC in the business of telling local affiliates that their licenses will be removed if they broadcast material that the FCC deems to be informationally false."
—Ben Shapiro, host, *The Ben Shapiro Show*

President Trump has announced his intention to nominate Brendan Carr, a Federal Communications Commission (FCC) commissioner, to become the agency's chairman after a quick Senate confirmation process.

Carr responded on social media, proclaiming, "We must dismantle the censorship cartel and restore free speech rights for everyday Americans."[1]

In a later post, he added, "Broadcast media have had the privilege of using a scarce and valuable public resource—our airwaves. In turn, they are required by law to operate in the public interest. When the transition is complete, the FCC will enforce this public interest obligation."[2]

The Foundation of Broadcast Regulation

Two core principles were established with the Communications Act of 1934 (which has been amended periodically and remains the charter for broadcast television today).

First, Congress prohibited common carriage for broadcasters and mandated a government-controlled, short-term licensing regime that assigned broadcasters to designated channels in the electromagnetic spectrum.

Second, to justify this exclusionary zoning policy, Congress also required that broadcasters act as trustees of the spectrum on behalf of all the others who were kept off the airwaves by the government. As guardians of a scarce and publicly owned resource, broadcasters must operate in the "public interest, convenience and necessity."

The Mystery of an Undefined Standard

The legislative history of the Radio Act of 1927, the precursor of the current Communications Act of 1934 that remains in force, does not explain the origins of the broadcast public interest standard. One explanation is that when the drafters reached an impasse in their attempt to define a standard, a young lawyer on loan to the Senate from the Interstate Commerce Commission suggested the words "public interest, convenience and necessity"—the standard used in the Interstate Commerce Act that created the Interstate Commerce Commission. The drafters agreed.

Although the FCC has relative freedom to regulate under the broadcast public interest standard, it is restricted from censorship or interfering with free speech under the First Amendment.

Current FCC Interpretation

The FCC has said that "our general mandate . . . calls for consideration of other factors and a balancing of all relevant factors by this Commission in assessing the public interest."[3] It has further clarified that the statutory duty to broadcast in the "public interest" imposes on licensees an obligation to be sensitive to problems of public concern in the community and to make sufficient time available for a complete discussion of such issues on a non-discriminatory basis.

The courts and the FCC have noted that "public interest" implies a balance of all relevant factors that the agency should consider.

However, the FCC and the courts have failed to build a body of precedent to give the public interest standard a concrete, durable meaning.

The Need for Clarity

This decades-long lack of clarity calls for more focused legislative attention to what decisional guidance should be delegated to the FCC. Absent any action in the coming Congress, which seems unlikely, the FCC under Chairman Carr can and should articulate a set of public interest principles that can be applied to broadcasting with greater transparency and consistency.

Only then can any pledge to pursue greater enforcement of violators be accepted as something more than mere political retribution, which Trump threatened repeatedly during his campaign. He proclaimed, "Commissioner Carr is a warrior for free speech."

The Jimmy Kimmel Controversy: A Case Study

In September 2025, these concerns moved from theoretical to actual when Chairman Carr's invocation of the public interest standard triggered a media firestorm. Following comedian Jimmy Kimmel's monologue comments about the alleged killer of conservative activist Charlie Kirk, Carr called Kimmel's remarks "the sickest conduct possible" and suggested that ABC affiliates continuing to air Kimmel's show might face FCC investigations for potential violations of their public interest obligations.

In a podcast interview, Carr told broadcasters: "We can do this the easy way or the hard way. These companies can find ways to change conduct and take actions on Kimmel, or there's going to be additional work for the FCC ahead."[4] The implication was clear: local stations licensed by the FCC could face regulatory scrutiny—potentially including challenges to their license renewals—if they continued airing content the chairman deemed contrary to the public interest.

Within hours of Carr's comments, major broadcast groups Nexstar and Sinclair—both with pending business before the FCC—announced they would preempt Kimmel's show on their ABC-affiliated stations.

ABC then suspended *Jimmy Kimmel Live!* indefinitely, though the show returned to air one week later, on September 24, 2025.

Carr later claimed that Kimmel's suspension resulted from "ratings, not because of anything that's happened at the federal government level," and that his comments were merely explaining the hypothetical complaint process. However, the sequence of events—from Carr's threats to affiliate preemption to network suspension, all within hours—suggested what legal scholars call "jawboning": government officials using implicit threats to compel private action without formal legal proceedings.

The Kimmel controversy starkly illustrates the danger of an undefined public interest standard in the hands of a politically motivated regulator. What constitutes serving the "public interest"? Political commentary the chairman agrees with? Entertainment that avoids offending the administration? The vagueness that has persisted since 1927 creates precisely the kind of arbitrary enforcement power that the First Amendment was designed to constrain.

Carr will now be able to demonstrate why he has earned his accolade as "a warrior for free speech." He can help lessen the palpable anxieties of broadcasters who fear that their futures as FCC licensees may be rocky if the "public interest" becomes a free speech cudgel instead of an enduring civic ideal. The anxieties generated by the Kimmel episode have transformed from abstract concerns into concrete realities.

CHAPTER 24

A Diminishing Electronic Media Future for Political Advertising (2017)

A mid a widening political rift between our two major political parties, an unusual philosophical bond was forged between them. President Trump, in 2020 re-election mode, already had a campaign apparatus in place. There was ample funding to produce pro-Trump advertising and to purchase time for these early campaign spots to run on major broadcast and cable networks, which reach a wide national audience. CNN and others, however, refused to air a paid spot since it contained a "fake news" label attached to mainstream media.

Not surprisingly, the blowback from the Trump campaign was intense. It said this refusal represented "a chilling precedent against free speech rights. . . . All of the mainstream media television networks have blocked the ad [celebrating] the achievements of President Trump in his first 100 days in office, including CNN, ABC, CBS, and NBC."[1]

Supreme Court Precedent

But nearly fifty years ago, the US Supreme Court established a durable legal precedent regarding this issue. In a seminal case, the Democratic National Committee formally requested that the Federal Communications Commission issue a declaratory ruling that, under the First Amendment and the Communications Act of 1934, refusing to sell time to solicit funds or comment on public issues was prohibited. The FCC rejected the DNC's argument, but its decision was reversed by the US Court of Appeals for the District of Columbia Circuit.

Three years later, the Supreme Court issued its own opinion in this case, reversing the decision of the appellate court and upholding the FCC's decision not to act. Chief Justice Warren Burger, a conservative jurist appointed by President Nixon, wrote an opinion that tipped the scales away from the notion that political speech holds the power to contribute to an informed electorate and back toward the principle of broadcaster discretion.

Here is the most powerful passage from that case:

> "Even though it would be in the public interest for the respondents' advertisements [a group called Business Executives Move for Vietnam Peace had sought to buy time for an anti-war ad] to be heard, it does not follow that the public interest requires every broadcaster to broadcast them. And it certainly does not follow that the public interest would be served by forcing every broadcaster to accept any particular kind of advertising."[2]

The Digital Migration

This precedent indicates that the government should have no role in mandating political advertising distribution in all mass media, including print, broadcast, and cable. This places the Trump campaign on an equal footing with the candidates and issues that the DNC chooses to support.

The case has also created an unintended consequence of promoting more political advertising online and on social media. Ironically, the Trump ad received widespread distribution there, including among President Trump's twenty-four million Twitter followers. It even received attention as a news item by some of the networks that refused to carry the spot.

Campaigns now can be expected to devote substantially larger advertising budgets to online and social media. According to the Pew Research Center, TV remains the most widely used platform, with 57 percent of American adults utilizing it as a news source. But 38 percent already get their news online, with most of this group accessing news websites, apps, and social media. Unlike broadcast or cable TV, there is no shortage of online outlets that will distribute spots that the major networks decline in the interest of exercising their own First Amendment rights.

At least in these digital domains, there seems to be no conflict between Republicans and Democrats, nor between free speech and the free market. Viewed in tandem, it's easy to understand that the barriers to entry and ever-increasing reach of online and social media will make the legal barriers to buying broadcast or cable TV time far less formidable over time.

PART VII

PRACTICAL STEPS TO SUPPORT FREE EXPRESSION

"The duty to defend the First Amendment does not rest with government, but with all of us. Free speech is the foundation of our democracy, and we must push back against any attempt to erode it."
—Federal Communications Commissioner Anna Gomez

"I'll fight any—any—attempt by the government to get involved with speech."
—US Senator Rand Paul (R-KY)

Constitutional principles matter only when citizens actively support them in daily life. Analysis that leads to action will require concrete steps that individuals, institutions, and communities can take to resist encroachment on the First Amendment while also strengthening a free expression culture.

CHAPTER 25

Free Speech, Free Press, Play Ball! (2023)

As Major League Baseball begins its season opening, let's add another tradition to America's treasured pastime—reciting the First Amendment before the game begins.

For decades, we have solemnly risen as the public address announcer intones, "Ladies and gentlemen, please join us as we sing 'The Star-Spangled Banner.'" Or in some cases, our attention is drawn to an opera star or pop singer who comes on the field to perform the national anthem, as we all mouth the words while waiting to see how high the last few notes will be belted out.

This ritual can be more than a hallowed tradition. It can speak to our pride as Americans, in "the land of the free and the home of the brave." Reciting a mere forty-five words right before—"Congress shall make no law respecting an establishment of religion or prohibiting the free exercise thereof; or abridging the freedom of speech, or of the press, or the right of the people peaceably to assemble, and to petition the government for a redress of grievances"—would provide more meaning to this cherished song.

Many people have sung the national anthem for years without any real appreciation for its significance in our country's historic fight to maintain vital constitutional freedoms, which remain the gold standard for the world. In recent weeks, we have witnessed the clampdown of free speech and press by Russia's Vladimir Putin with understandable horror, reminding us of the red line that is required to have democracy prevail over autocracy.

Reciting the First Amendment before "The Star-Spangled Banner" can create a greater sense of unity in our highly polarized country, too, since it transcends political party affiliation or leanings. That's because the First Amendment serves all Americans, and as such, should be celebrated before each game by everyone. It also would remind us that if players and coaches decide to kneel in protest when the national anthem is played, they are doing so in reverence to free speech protections that enable them to express themselves without fear of any government reprisals.

And for those who think the words will be too difficult to remember without an accompanying tune, it's easy to flash them on the stadium Jumbotron. Problem solved.

At a time when government prohibitions on what can be read in classrooms seem to be re-emerging, and as the safety of journalists increasingly is being threatened, beginning each MLB game with a recital of the First Amendment would represent a powerful affirmation, in the stands and among TV viewers, of our core constitutional values.

It would represent the perfect prelude to singing "The Star-Spangled Banner," and no doubt would pump up the crowd even more as part of the anticipation of the two words that everyone always waits for with great anticipation. "Play Ball!"

CHAPTER 26

The First Amendment Should Be the Next Movie Blockbuster (2022)

If you've been to a movie theater recently, you might notice that the ticket lines are longer, the refreshments are more expensive, and the number of commercials before the coming attractions is more plentiful. The data clearly explain this surge in moviegoing now that people are back in the habit of going to theaters after the COVID-19 shutdown. Summer revenue was at $1.96 billion through July 4, up nearly 200 percent from the same period in 2021, according to the analytics firm ComScore.

Given the vast number of Americans from every walk of life who now are assembled many times every day and night in their local cinemas, perhaps there is an opportunity to create a greater common understanding about the bedrock democratic principle that we all share—the First Amendment, which covers freedom of religious thought and practice; freedom of speech; freedom of the press; freedom of assembly; and freedom to petition government about grievances.

Here, the data is far less encouraging. For example, a recent Knight Foundation survey found that less than half of high school teachers and students included in its nationwide sample supported the notion that freedom of speech should be supported when it is "offensive" or "threatening." Notions about freedom of the press are only slightly higher—57 percent indicated that news organizations should be able to publish without government censorship.[1]

Seeing the forty-five words of the First Amendment appear on the screen before any commercials or coming attractions are shown could represent a great national civics lesson for moviegoers of all ages. And to add a little pizzazz, what about having Tom Cruise, Thor, or even the Minions recite the First Amendment in a brief film clip right after the lights are dimmed?

Bringing the First Amendment into movie theaters as a regular part of the cinema experience could create a greater sense of unity in our highly polarized country, too, since it transcends political party affiliation or leanings. That's because the First Amendment serves all Americans and should be celebrated before each screening by everyone.

CHAPTER 27

Media Literacy for Democracy's Next Generation (2021)

A First-in-the-Nation Law

Although the tidal wave of misinformation continues unabated, the new year has already seen one ray of hope. In early January, New Jersey Governor Phil Murphy signed the first-in-the-nation law that requires public schools to teach media literacy at all grade levels, K-12.

Murphy noted in his signing statement, "Our democracy remains under sustained attack through the proliferation of misinformation that is eroding the role of truth in our political and civic discourse. It is our responsibility to ensure our nation's future leaders are equipped with the tools necessary to identify fact from fiction."

In the law, the state Board of Education is charged with developing media-literacy standards that must include researching, using critical thinking skills, and learning the difference between facts and opinions, and primary and secondary sources. Public hearings will also be held as part of this standards development process.

Translating Virtues into Tangible Outcomes

Here are a few suggested areas that can translate the law's virtues into tangible outcomes:

Integration Across All Subjects

First, it's important that media literacy become integrated across all subject areas, rather than just taught as a unit of a particular subject area, such as social studies. Misinformation respects no disciplinary boundaries: it can proliferate in news about current events, science, technology, or any other field where fast-moving developments can foster half-baked ideas, rumors, conspiracy theories, or outright lies.

Experiential Learning Over Theory

Teaching media literacy should also veer away from theoretical lectures in favor of experiential learning designed for suitability at various age levels. Students should gain an increasingly sophisticated sense of media information discernment as they move through elementary, middle, and high school, which is best accomplished by having them explore real-life problems individually and collectively in a classroom setting.

Training Teachers for Success

Better training for teachers to undertake hands-on media literacy training should also be part of making any new standards meaningful. This vital aspect will need to be supported by local school boards allocating sufficient financial resources and providing time off for teachers to be taught media literacy themselves. More senior faculty members need to accelerate their understanding of the complexities of social media to teach current and future generations of digital natives. Growing up with legacy media such as newspapers and broadcast television won't be very relevant since, for the most part, media literacy really means social media literacy to anyone enrolled in public school today.

Learning from International Models

And it will be important for New Jersey to build upon the successes other countries have had in rolling out effective media-literacy education on a massive scale. The current gold standard is Finland, which begins its instruction even earlier—in preschool. The Finnish approach provides teachers with wide latitude in how they incorporate media literacy in their lesson plans, which means that teachers can tailor their instruction to create real student engagement rather than merely drill them on passing standards-developed exams. The results? Finland now ranks first among European countries for resilience to misinformation, according to an Open Society Institute survey. Norway, Denmark, Estonia, Ireland, and Sweden are other countries of note that can be looked at as New Jersey's media-literacy standards are developed.[1]

Extending Learning Beyond the Classroom

Finally, although starting early has real upsides, the massive population of those long gone from public schools should not be left out entirely. Here, Finland again can serve as a model, since it has begun to take advantage of the best media-literacy practices developed by teachers, adapting them for adults through public libraries. This community outreach can and should be done throughout the Garden State, as well, to demonstrate that what works in Helsinki can also work in Hackensack, Hightstown, or Ho-Ho-Kus.

With effective implementation, the New Jersey law can be more than just a step in the right direction, helping to create better-informed citizens over time. Students (and ideally their parents and grandparents, too) should be equipped with lifelong tools to help them deal with the information tsunami that surely will continue throughout the years ahead.

CHAPTER 28

Guardrails for Fake News, Misinformation, and Disinformation (2021)

――――――

Perhaps the most distasteful national omelet we've been served in recent years has been the one that has mixed an unsavory combination of three ingredients: fake news, misinformation, and disinformation.

While many express growing concerns and look for ways to deal with them, that may be difficult if we use these terms without any agreed-upon definitions that set useful boundaries and are easy to understand among the public at large. The alternative is to continue repeating the mantra "fake news-misinformation-disinformation" so often that it loses meaning, or using the terms interchangeably so that they become permanently blurred in our minds.

Defining Fake News

"Fake news" should refer to a communication in any format—print, video, or online—but only if generated by the news media itself, which is comprised of professional journalists who have chosen the career path of reporting. This starting point would delimit vast amounts of information from meeting this definition, so it could not simply be applied to any communication by anyone.

Doctors are part of the medical community, lawyers are part of the legal community, and journalists are part of the news community.

How many times have you heard someone say fake medicine when they disagreed with a diagnosis or fake law when they disagreed with a legal argument? Fake news should be equally rare.

The Associated Press is an excellent baseline. It's an independent global news organization dedicated to factual reporting, founded in 1846. More than half of the world's population sees AP journalism every day, with reporting from 250 locations worldwide. About fifteen thousand news outlets are part of this AP community, and all of them should be considered as a bona fide news medium. Conversely, if they are not in the AP universe, it may be inaccurate and unfair to refer to any other source of communication as fake news.

Understanding Misinformation

Misinformation is perhaps the largest category at issue. I think any communication on social media—from anyone to anyone—may wind up being called misinformation if it is inaccurate in any way. Yet that would be too broad-brushed an approach.

We tend to thrive on sending and receiving gossip, rumors, and even biting satire that surely is not intended to be judged for its accuracy. So misinformation should be limited to a smaller subset that is based on information that relies on verifiable data rather than opinions.

Misinformation is really mistaken information, and it's not essential to characterize the source as benign or malignant to have that information corrected. The problem in social media is that a cry of misinformation too often turns into a finger-pointing exercise aimed at denigrating the motives of the person who communicated it.

When the battle cry goes out, anyone who characterizes a post as misinformation should be prepared to point out the nature of the mistake and provide a correction. This would help minimize the weaponization of the characterization to demonize or demean the conveyor of that information.

Identifying Disinformation

This descriptive category, like misinformation, should also be applied specifically to social media. In contrast, it should be focused on foreign governments and groups working on their behalf, which have the intent of providing misleading information that is designed to create confusion or dissension in our electoral process or in aspects of national security.

The behavior of these bad actors is really the central issue here, so concrete responses by the United States are the best way to combat this threat to democratic norms. This will require robust governmental offensive and defensive measures through diplomatic channels, including targeted counter-disinformation campaigns and sanctions when specific cases of disinformation arise. The purveyors of disinformation are largely known, including Russia, Iran, North Korea, and China, along with terrorist organizations.

Looking Ahead

My proposal of a new classification system for these three concepts is illustrative rather than comprehensive, and I hope that it will be refined through a broader discussion within our communities of interest. The best first step will be to recognize that the labels being applied to these widespread communication phenomena need corresponding definitional guardrails if we are to develop the types of effective, tailored responses that each area requires.

CHAPTER 29

The Two Questions That Can Save Us from Digital Deception

We sit with our laptops, tablets, and smartphones, fingers twitching in anticipation as we scour our emails, bookmarks, and social media pages to see what we've missed since last logging on—even if that was only a few minutes ago. We click, then link, like, and repeat.

The Web Is Like Whisper Down the Lane

Of course, there's no harm in sending or receiving dozens of YouTube cat videos or blooper clips from local morning talk shows. But as we mine the web for news and information that influences how we vote, what we buy, or even how we diagnose our medical symptoms, we often find ourselves in a perpetual version of that wonderful childhood game, Telephone. That's where someone starts a conversation, whispers it to another, and it goes down the line until the last person blurts out what he or she heard. What makes it so comical is that it usually bears only a faint resemblance to what the original speaker said or meant.

The web is like Telephone on steroids. By the time we process and repeat information gleaned from it—whether online or at the water cooler—we may have only the slightest memory of where we first encountered it. Even if we do, we often have little way to understand its veracity or context. The phrase "I saw it on the internet" is all too often uttered as reassurance that if something appears online, it must be both real and worth repeating.

The Internet's Abundance of Information Can Still Fall Short of Reliable Facts

This concern has larger public policy implications as well. For example, a recent *New York Times* piece summarizing a forthcoming *Virginia Law Review* article by Professor Allison Orr Larsen, a College of William & Mary law professor, illustrates that in a growing number of cases, the US Supreme Court reflects this same unfortunate phenomenon. "Some of the factual assertions in recent amicus briefs would not pass muster in a high school research paper. But that has not stopped the Supreme Court from relying on them. Recent opinions have cited 'facts' from amicus briefs that were backed up by blog posts, emails, or nothing at all."[1]

Years ago, in another context, my colleague Newton Minow (the former FCC chairman who famously said that television was a "vast wasteland") offered me a pearl of wisdom that I think about whenever I'm online, sending or receiving something that affects how I think or act. He taught me the importance of two questions that now have special resonance in our digital lives:

> *How do you know that?*
> *What does that mean?*

A Credible Source

The first question deals with what journalists or law enforcement officers might term a credible source. Where does what you're reading or viewing come from? Is it based on a reliable firsthand account or something someone relayed in a "game" of Telephone? If facts are presented, where did they come from? If an opinion is advanced, what is the basis for it?

Context Matters

The second question assumes that this initial credibility bar has been met. It focuses on what the source was trying to convey. Is this something to be taken at face value? Or is it communicating a different meaning by using ambiguous words that are subject to multiple interpretations? And if so, which of these meanings is the most plausible one? Of course, this question is also useful as a snark filter, since so much of what we respond to and share with others is ironic or, as many would say, post-ironic.

Much of the web's future, both commercially and otherwise, will be built around the idea of curation—finding and relying on aggregation sources that we know and like. These may help us manage an otherwise endless flood of information for rapid consumption, but the two questions, slightly changed, still are worth posing, whether for the *Huffington Post*, *BBC News*, *TMZ*, or another online outlet: How do they know that? What do they mean?

Individually and collectively—including in our halls of power— these two questions will help us feel more centered in thinking about the veracity of what we read or watch online. It's useful to remember them along with your password before you log on again today.

CHAPTER 30

America Needs a National News Council Once Again (2025)

"The United States is now passing through an era marked by divisive, often bitter, social conflict. New groups have coalesced to assault the privileges of the established; new ideas have arisen to challenge the validity of the old. Stridency and partisanship, militancy and defiance are in the air."

Although this is an apt summary of American political and social malaise today, that sobering perspective was conveyed over fifty years ago in *A Free and Responsive Press: The Twentieth Century Fund Task Force Report for a National News Council.*[1]

The findings there, sadly, have withstood the test of time. "Disaffection with existing institutions, prevalent in every sector of society, has spread to the media of public information—newspapers and magazines, radio and television. Their accuracy, fairness and responsibility have come under challenge. The media have found their credibility questioned, their freedom threatened, by public officials whose own credibility depends on the very media they threaten."

And the ominous consequences have moved well beyond hypothetical scenarios to current realities. As the task force report noted, "A free society cannot endure without a free press, and the freedom of the press ultimately rests on public understanding of, and trust in its work. The public, as well as the press, has a vital interest in enhancing the credibility of the media and in protecting their freedom of expression. One barrier to credibility is the absence in this country of any established national and independent mechanism for hearing complaints about the media or for examining issues concerning freedom of the press."

This foundational thinking led to the creation of the National News Council in 1973. But the Council dissolved in 1984 after eleven years of operations, attributing its demise to "a general lack of news media acceptance of the concept of a news council."

In the announcement of its closure, its chairman, former CBS News President Richard S. Salant, was prescient in observing that while that organization would cease its activities, the need for its existence would continue. "The press itself in coming years will reach the same conclusion," he noted.

Bill Arthur, the News Council's founding executive director, commented, "I fully expect that the day will come when the press of our nation [print and broadcast] will cry out in the wilderness for an organization such as the one we have served."[2]

Having served on the staff of the National News Council as a Matthew H. Fox Fellow in Law and Journalism a long time ago in a galaxy far, far away—and as the only still-active media professional with first-hand knowledge of its operating practices and pitfalls—I find myself in a unique position to make the case why a new National News Council is needed now more than ever.

In doing so, I also recognize the failures of the original version, which can provide important practical lessons that need to be addressed if the concept is worthy of further development.

Confronting Declining News Media Trust

Fast forward to 2025 and beyond. Today's news media—in print, broadcasting, cable, and, increasingly, online—are caught between a rock and a hard place. At one end is an ever-expanding demonization of the press by senior government officials and others. Accusations of "fake news" now are routinely made at the highest ranks of elected and appointed officials—attracting headlines, clickbait, and even, in some cases, expensive and time-consuming litigation.

In September 2025, Gallup reported that Americans' confidence in the mass media has edged down to a new low.[3] When Gallup began measuring trust in the news media in the 1970s, between 68 percent and 72 percent of Americans expressed confidence in reporting. However, by the next reading in 1997, public confidence had fallen to 53 percent. Media trust remained just above 50 percent until it dropped to 44 percent in 2004, and it has not risen to the majority level since then.

Its latest national survey data indicates that fewer than three in ten Americans—28 percent—now place trust in newspapers, television, and radio to report the news fully, fairly, and accurately. Additionally, this decline is evident across all major voting groups, including Republicans, Democrats, and Independents. Generational divides also underscore the erosion; older adults hold significantly more faith in the news media than younger Americans.

Gallup's conclusion deserves close attention: "[T]he challenge for news organizations is not only to deliver fair and accurate reporting but also to regain credibility across an increasingly polarized and skeptical public."

According to the Pew Research Center, "Midway through the twentieth century, the news media were among the most trusted institutions in the United States. Today, it sits near the bottom of the list, outflanked only by Congress in most surveys. . . . Everybody knows the media has a credibility problem. And seemingly everyone has got a beef with the news."[4]

There now is an endless loop dynamic—increasing public policy pressure to crack down on news media in formal and informal ways while fueling cynicism from American news consumers across generations. That loop needs to be severed, if possible, with some fresh thinking about how the news media can help break such a damaging and self-reinforcing cycle.

Searching for a Better Pathway

Political scientist Jonathan Ladd argues, in *Why Americans Hate the Media and How It Matters*, that industry insiders too often embrace the notion that a trusted, independent prestige press is the natural order of things.[5] In fact, before the twentieth century, few news organizations fit the definition of a prestige press, and many had partisan agendas.

Ladd writes that in this historical context, the so-called golden age of American journalism that gave us the Pentagon Papers and the Watergate investigation is more of an anomaly than the status quo. He also indicates that news leaders fall prey to the myth that trust used to be high because journalists were especially competent at their jobs decades ago. In fact, trust was high for a variety of reasons, including the low-choice media environment, as well as a more forgiving political culture.

Jesse Holcomb, the former principal adviser to the Trust, Media, and Democracy project at the Knight Foundation, observed, "The news industry needs to reckon with these myths. To be clear-eyed about the way forward, it needs to be clear-eyed about its past. But reckoning is only one part of the strategy."[6]

A free press is essential to democracy—full stop. Ralph Otwell, the late former managing editor of the *Chicago Sun-Times*, noted that the chief purpose of the First Amendment "was simply to further enable democracy to work—the idea being that an unfettered press would inform and lead the citizens to make the best choices in their own best interests. The press was given the role of a mere agent of the people, a conduit for information, a vehicle for letting the truth win its way. . . . If the public finds no truth to believe, no press to trust, no credible agent of information, then the whole system would collapse, and we would again be at the mercy of a repressive government."[7]

A 2020 Pew Research Center survey found that three-fourths of Americans believe it's possible to improve public confidence in the media.[8] So, what can news organizations do to repair relationships with their most skeptical audiences? In simple terms, it's especially timely to explore the possibility of a National News Council 2.0 as one way forward.

Focusing on First Principles

What would be the essential principles for a National News Council 2.0 to convey? Let's start with:

The importance of robust opinion

Provided there are no significantly misleading statements, the news media should be encouraged to take forthright stands on controversial subjects, promoting editorial views with vigor and supporting them with facts they deem relevant and persuasive.

While the news media are entitled to very considerable latitude in determining which facts to stress and which to play down or totally ignore, the limits of robust opinion journalism are exceeded when distortions and misrepresentations occur, producing an overall effect that can be perceived as seriously misleading.

Opinion journalism should be viewed broadly, allowing for the broadest possible latitude in the presentation of a point of view. But when dealing with controversial subjects, the expression of a point of view should be supported by facts that, at the very least, are consistent with that viewpoint.

The public's right to know the facts

While minor errors may arise, care should be taken to see that condensation in the creation of a news story does not result in misleading the public in any significant way. Statements taken out of context may carry implications when standing alone that would be rebutted, directly or indirectly, in a more complete rendition.

Care should be taken in the editing of a news account that contains quotations to see that necessary explanations are not omitted and that the quotation is not presented in such a way as to distort the intent of the person being quoted.

When the news media show enterprise by publishing a news account based on information gathered from sources before the release of an official report, they should be careful to review the official report, once released, to see if it corroborates the earlier information. If it does not, the news media have an obligation to their readers and viewers to inform them of the inconsistencies or the content of the full report.

Extreme care should be taken in presenting news accounts of scientific or medical research to avoid making such research appear more conclusive than it is.

When reporters are denied access to official sources, they are entitled to draw reasonable inferences from the facts available if the report is not made inaccurate in any material element. Interpretive reporting should, however, be labeled as such.

If the significance of the reported facts could be better understood with a further explanation from official sources, even though such further explanation is received after publication of the original story, that explanation should be made available to the public.

When using the statistical results of technical studies as support for various conclusions, journalists should be careful that the statistics are consistent with the initial premises.

The use of unnamed sources

Although a reporter is not required to reveal sources in a news account, the use of such confidential sources places a greater responsibility on a news organization to determine that the source does not use anonymity as a platform from which to dispense incorrect information with impunity. A news organization is remiss when it relies heavily on unidentified sources and then refuses to make public refutations from the persons named in a news story.

Establishing National News Council 2.0 Procedures

A twenty-first-century National News Council, unlike its predecessor, should be modest in its aspirations and operating procedures. It cannot resolve all the problems facing the news media, nor will it answer all the criticisms voiced by politicians and the public. However, it could be an independent body to which the public can take complaints about press coverage. It could act as a strong defender of press freedom, attempt to make the media accountable to the public, and lessen the tensions between the press and the government.

Several threshold operating procedures are worth considering:

- Individuals and organizations should be allowed to bring complaints to the Council. The Council should also be able to initiate inquiries into any situation where governmental action threatens freedom of the press.

- Any complainant should try to resolve the grievance with the media organization involved before the Council initiates any action on a complaint.
- Complainants should be required to waive the right to legal proceedings in court on any matter taken up in Council proceedings. This will provide an alternative forum for dispute resolution and could minimize frivolous or time-consuming litigation.
- The Council's processes, findings, and conclusions should not be employed by government agencies, including the Federal Communications Commission in its decisions on broadcast license renewals.
- Most importantly, all Council findings should be made available to the public as widely as possible, utilizing a variety of mass media and social media platforms as soon as findings are made.

Learning from Failure

The failure of the first National News Council should not be a barrier to exploring the creation of a new one. But the reasons for its demise are well documented and should be accounted for as fresh thinking is developed, including how to avoid past pitfalls.

As Patrick Brogan noted in the Council's 1985 book-length autopsy, *Spiked: The Short Life and Death of the National News Council*: "If a news council is ever reestablished, it clearly will have to solve its financial problems first. . . . The News Council itself was funded with grants from two foundations and never recovered when they ran out."[9]

If the past is prologue, it is unlikely that the news media itself will support a new News Council in its early days, at least not until the memory of the former Council's failure has faded.

Brogan also correctly indicated, "A News Council must not, I believe, depend upon the goodwill of the press. It must always be ready to criticize newspapers or television, even those that contribute to its costs."[10]

On the other hand, news media financial support, with limited amounts for any individual news organization, should be welcomed. Brogan's rationale here is spot on again. "If its members are not ready, instantly and on the least provocation, to bite the hand that feeds them, then they clearly are in the wrong line of business."

Critically, rather than recreating a financial and operational model based on the big thinking of the 1970s, a new National News Council can and should modestly adhere to the maxim "less is more."

Regarding necessary start-up expenses that exceed what foundations and the news media will contribute, in our current world of crowdfunding, there are now efficient new ways to generate both short-term and ongoing operational funds through thousands of small tax-deductible donations on digital platforms, such as Donorbox and Fundly.

A new Council also should not need rent high-priced offices in New York City nor build up a high-salaried staff with expensive overhead. With today's virtual organizations that take full advantage of AI's ever-expanding capabilities, it will be relatively easy for a small group of seasoned employees to manage a caseload of complaints, even if they are voluminous.

In-depth research for complaints that satisfy screening requirements could also be undertaken without expending large amounts of human labor. Some of the nation's top journalism and media schools, for example, could be invited to regularly provide AI-savvy graduate student interns supervised by faculty members with deep news media professional backgrounds. Such supplementary resources would be a win-win for both the Council and the participating institutions.

As before, the Council itself would also meet periodically to review the staff findings and vote on whether to accept, reject, or modify them. Members would not be compensated for contributing time to such a worthy public mission, which is the norm for those who agree to serve on boards of nonprofit organizations.

Admittedly, there may be controversy about how Council members are appointed and whether they bring an unacceptable level of bias to their roles, unable to evaluate alleged news media transgressions objectively. But in a larger sense, our legal system has been able to function well for over two hundred years when qualified jurors are empaneled for civil and criminal trials. This problem may not be as insurmountable as it seems at first glance.

As before, some Council members should be current or former news media professionals, given their deep knowledge and experience. Others should come from academia, the ranks of respected former judges, or leaders in the private or public sectors.

Even in these polarized times, it should be possible to assemble a respected group of a dozen or so Council members who a broad swath of the public will perceive as credible individuals whose judgments are worth considering. If not, we are in a deeper state of societal dysfunction that is truly alarming.

The immediacy and universal availability of social media also represent powerful attributes that were not available a half-century ago. The low visibility of the original National News Council's work, which contributed to its demise, now would be obsolete.

The Council's findings on viral social media blasts would reach millions within minutes, then become amplified exponentially through reposting and mass media coverage. Assertions of "fake news" would be able to be confirmed or refuted by the Council, which would help diminish the rhetorical power of that unfortunate catchphrase.

In turn, this may help instill greater trust in news media and more measured attacks by others who lack factual bases for making them.

The Road Ahead

Alas, it's time to admit that the news media's main line of defense is not the Constitution. Instead, it is public support and trust that must be constantly earned.

A reimagined National News Council would not be a silver bullet. However, it could help the news media prove that they deserve to be free and that their freedom protects fundamental democratic values, requiring additional support in our all-too-trying times.

PART VIII
GLOBAL PERSPECTIVES

———

Free expression around the world has steadily eroded. Increasingly, there are major obstacles to internet access, onerous restrictions on content, or serious violations of user rights in the form of unchecked surveillance or unjust repercussions for legitimate speech and reporting.

CHAPTER 31

Technologies of Freedom, Revisited (2014)

I received an invitation from former FCC Commissioner Robert McDowell to serve on an advisory council at The Media Institute that he is chairing. This new initiative, the Global Free Speech and Internet Program, will promote the internet as an "open and interoperable platform, largely free from government intrusion, where information can be shared freely." In that spirit, it will push back against international efforts to promote a government-centric model of internet governance.

My response was twofold. First, I accepted with enthusiasm, since this is a global public policy issue that I'm passionate about; it's one where US leadership has a continuing vital role to play. But as soon as I sent my email response, I logged off and went to my bookshelf. There, right where I knew it would be, was my well-worn copy of *Technologies of Freedom*, authored by my late cherished friend and colleague, Professor Ithiel de Sola Pool.[1]

Learning from a Global Pioneer

When I served at the National Telecommunications and Information Administration (NTIA), Ithiel would drop by whenever he was in Washington, D.C. He spent an hour or so with me learning about which new communication technologies were on the horizon, and how policymakers were thinking about them. These meetings always had a surreal quality, since I was a recent law school graduate and was tutoring an eminent professor who founded the Department of Political Science at MIT.

A few years later, I moved up to Cambridge, Massachusetts, and called Professor Pool to let him know I now was his neighbor. By then, he had established the Research Program on Communications Policy at MIT and organized a monthly MIT Communications Forum to explore many of the ideas that we had talked about in my office at NTIA.

Fortunately for me, and more importantly for the world at large, Ithiel subsequently decided to capture his thoughts in a manuscript about the brave new world of communication technologies as they met the brave old world of government controls over freedom of expression.

Timeless Warnings

I began flipping the pages of his book, which were littered with Post-It notes in various sections.

"Judges and legislators," Professor Pool wrote, "have tried to fit technological innovations under conventional legal concepts. The errors of understanding by these scientific laymen, though honest, have been mammoth. They have sought to guide toward good purposes technologies they did not comprehend."

He continued:

"Historically, the various media that are now converging have been differently organized and differently treated under the law. The outcome to be feared is that communications in the future may be unnecessarily regulated under the unfree tradition of law that has been applied so far to the electronic media. The clash between the print, common carrier, and broadcast models is likely to be a vehement communications policy issue in the next decades. Convergence of modes is upsetting the trifurcated system developed over the past two hundred years, and questions that had seemed to be settled centuries ago are being reopened, unfortunately sometimes not in a libertarian way."[2]

Reasons for Hope

These words might seem like those of an eternal pessimist, but Ithiel's conclusion in the book reflects just the opposite:

"The easy access, low cost, and distributed intelligence of modern means of communication are a prime reason for hope. . . . As long as the First Amendment stands, backed by courts that take it seriously, the loss of liberty is not foreordained. The commitment of American culture to pluralism and individual rights is reason for optimism, as is the pliancy and profusion of electronic technology."[3]

And then I remembered that *Technologies of Freedom* was published in 1983, and a year later, Ithiel de Sola Pool died after completing this seminal work. But his memory endures, his voice remains strong. The challenges that he framed remain alive for another generation to grapple with, as the pressures for greater government control of the internet loom ahead once more— both at home and abroad.

CHAPTER 32

Sending a Strong Signal on Global Internet Freedom (2017)

A mong the range of complex foreign policy issues yet to be addressed by recent administrations is a serious concern for global internet freedom. The growing restrictions on internet freedom around the world are easy to document; less so any visible American strategy that would reverse the ominous trends at hand.

Let's review the dimensions of the problem in brief. The latest data from the respected nonprofit organization, Freedom House, provides a contextual understanding, based on tracking global internet freedom in sixty-five countries, comprising 88 percent of internet users worldwide.[1]

According to its most recent annual report in this area, "Freedom on the Net," two-thirds of the world's internet users live under government censorship. Internet freedom around the world declined for the sixth consecutive year.

The Global Challenge

The types of blocked content include political communication aimed at promoting democratic values, such as online petitions and calls for public protests. Even satire can be punished severely: a twenty-two-year-old in Egypt was imprisoned for three years after photoshopping Mickey Mouse ears on President Abdel Fattah el-Sisi. Unfortunately, this type of criminal penalty is hardly unique.

Overall, Freedom House deemed only seventeen surveyed countries to have real internet freedom; twenty-eight were partly free and twenty were characterized as not free. The leading bad state actors should not be surprising: China, Syria, Iran, Ethiopia, Uzbekistan, and Cuba (North Korea was not included in the survey, alas).

Previous administrations had mixed success promoting global internet freedom. They provided modest funding through grant programs, with most monies given to provide technology for bloggers and dissidents in select restricted countries. But the same tools that protect freedom of expression online can also hide drug traffickers and child pornographers. And damaging leaks of highly classified NSA data by Edward Snowden hurt the United States as it advocated for greater internet freedom, since the notion of centralized government surveillance undercut the message that our nation intended to convey.

The Stakes for America

Despite these setbacks, there was a recognition at the highest levels of government that restricting global internet freedom was a growing problem. Less freedom would have enormous potential consequences for dealing with authoritarian regimes and diminish promising communication and ecommerce capabilities of an open global internet.

As technology expands these possibilities, many governments have placed greater restrictions on innovative new digital services. Freedom House has documented arrests for "misuse" of Facebook in twenty-seven countries, of YouTube in eleven countries, and of Twitter in nine countries. These are sobering numbers that current and future administrations will have difficulty ignoring, if only because internet freedom can affect both national security interests and trade imbalance concerns. The US would be hurt if the marketplace of ideas and the online commercial marketplace that thrives here were diminished overseas.

A Path Forward

However, there has been inconsistent leadership on this issue from recent administrations. Future Secretaries of State should provide both symbolism and substance for a new US global internet freedom agenda in high-profile addresses that echo the words of Hillary Clinton in a January 2010 speech at the Newseum: "This is a very important speech on a very important subject."

This phrase alone would send a strong diplomatic signal to the international community that the United States still considers internet freedom to be a critical area of foreign policy engagement. Equally important, it would mark the start of an updated internet freedom agenda based on success metrics and aimed at reversing the all-too-apparent downward spiral of repression.

The Need for Action

It's also timely for the United States to initiate a new internet freedom resolution before the UN General Assembly. Given the US global leadership role in internet apps, content, and devices, it remains in our national security and economic interest to formulate concrete steps to advance such a resolution in an assertive and practical context.

The United States should focus on mandates that countries would need to adopt within a reasonable time frame as a carrot, with the prospect of formal UN condemnation as a stick.

Under such an approach, all countries would need to develop transparent measures that prevent the intentional disruption of access to, or dissemination of, information online in violation of internet human rights law. These measures would need to ensure the protection of online freedom of expression, freedom of association, and privacy. A US-led resolution should require the adoption of national internet-related public policies that, at their core, are designed to promote universal online access.

Multilateral Approaches

In addition to improving the United Nations' current approach to internet freedom, the United States should also pursue other multilateral and bilateral activities to supplement and complement what can be accomplished at the United Nations. The Department of State should address internet freedom concerns in US foreign aid decisions. Our nation's influential role at the World Bank provides a potential range of possibilities for US foreign aid influence, as well. For example, the US could provide seed funding to establish an internet freedom trust fund that is administered by the World Bank, with specific investment priorities that reflect internet freedom concerns.

The current World Bank Digital Foundations Project in Malawi illustrates the type of project that would deserve funding by such a trust fund. It is designed to increase access to affordable, high-quality internet services for government, businesses, and citizens and to improve the government's capacity to deliver digital public services. The benefits of digital technology are aimed at reaching all citizens and helping lay the groundwork for growth of the digital economy. This is just the type of environment that can serve as the foundation for internet freedom, since it can attain broad political support within a country.

Building Partnerships

There also may be opportunities to influence internet freedom laws and policies within the context of bilateral negotiations (e.g., in international trade agreements). The United States can coordinate more closely with our tech private sector to leverage its power to influence internet laws and policies within restrictive countries. And our nation is well-positioned to assist countries in developing more effective data protection and privacy regimes that address consumer protection concerns (e.g., preserving anonymity to enhance freedom of expression).

Internet freedom is a bipartisan concern that can be promoted through a robust policy toolkit. It's finally time for the United States to develop more effective measures to influence its promotion and expansion around the world.

CHAPTER 33

Ukraine War's Powerful First Amendment Lesson (2022)

As Americans, we are witnessing the horror that Russia is inflicting on Ukraine with its bloody invasion that is causing massive devastation and death throughout the country. Ironically, the tragic events abroad can also help us gain a greater appreciation for the democratic values that we enjoy at home—values that Ukraine would like to emulate as it struggles to remain a democratic country.

That's because the proverbial Iron Curtain has been fortified by Vladimir Putin as a barrier against the Russian people. The populace there now is experiencing an unprecedented news and information crackdown by the government, which is shutting off outside news media and social media outlets or causing them to leave the country. As BBC director-general Tim Davie noted in a statement, "This legislation appears to criminalize the process of independent journalism. . . . It leaves us no other option than to temporarily suspend the work of all BBC News journalists within the Russian Federation while we assess the full implications of this unwelcome development." Russian citizens who have taken to the streets in protest of Putin's unwarranted siege also face the prospect of long jail sentences.[1]

The Dangerous Power of Government Repression

Taken together, these measures starkly illustrate that government power can be overwhelming when applied to freedom of speech and freedom of the press.

Our nation's founders wisely could foresee the dangers of misapplied government power, thus necessitating constitutional limits that enable free expression and transparency to help us find out about governmental deeds and misdeeds. The democratic ideals of our nation would not be possible to achieve without these restraints.

When the Bill of Rights was enacted in 1789 and ratified by the states in 1791, it included a First Amendment that prohibited Congress (and in effect, all government legislators and regulators) from restricting freedom of speech and freedom of the press. Aside from some narrow exceptions, such as obscenity and defamation, the First Amendment has endured and even expanded in recent years through various Supreme Court decisions.

Learning from Global Events

The Russian response to the Ukrainian war it initiated should make all of us better understand that the fundamental nature of the First Amendment is to serve as a firewall and heat shield from government speech and press restrictions.

Putin's malign news and information measures demonstrate that the wrath of government can wreak as much havoc as an artillery of tanks or a truckload full of grenades.

We should pay close attention to what is happening in Moscow to maintain vigilance in safeguarding the vital stakes of our own freedoms.

PART IX

THE PATH FORWARD

Indifference and ignorance are no longer sustainable. A nation where many citizens cannot name the rights that protect their freedom, where trust in media has collapsed along partisan lines, and where young people increasingly see shouting down speakers or blocking debate as acceptable behavior is a nation losing its capacity for self-correction. The surveys don't just reveal troubling data—they reveal a society forgetting how to disagree without destroying, how to debate without demonizing, how to remain free without descending into chaos. A free expression path forward is necessary not because democracy is fragile in theory, but because it's failing in practice when citizens abandon the courage and commitment it requires for the long term.

CHAPTER 34

The Enduring Wisdom of US Supreme Court Justices Brandeis and Holmes

This passage from Justice Brandeis's historic concurrence in *Whitney v. California*, joined by Justice Holmes, stands as one of the most eloquent defenses of First Amendment freedoms ever written, offering wisdom that remains vital nearly a century later. It articulates a profound philosophy: that the founders understood free speech not merely as a right to be tolerated, but as essential infrastructure for democratic self-governance. We must continue to have a deep faith in citizens' capacity for reasoned judgment when given access to competing ideas, while recognizing that attempts to silence dissent often backfire, breeding the very fear, repression, and instability they aim to prevent.

"Those who won our independence believed that the final end of the state was to make men free to develop their faculties, and that in its government the deliberative forces should prevail over the arbitrary. They valued liberty both as an end and as a means. They believed liberty to be the secret of happiness and courage to be the secret of liberty. They believed that freedom to think as you will and to speak as you think are means indispensable to the discovery and spread of political truth; that without free speech and assembly discussion would be futile; that with them, discussion affords ordinarily adequate protection against the dissemination of noxious doctrine; that the greatest menace to freedom is an inert people; that public discussion is a political duty; and that this should be a fundamental principle of the American government. They recognized the risks to which all human institutions are subject. But they knew that order cannot be secured merely through fear of punishment for its infraction; that it is hazardous to discourage thought, hope and imagination; that fear breeds repression; that repression breeds hate; that hate menaces stable government; that the path of safety lies in the opportunity to discuss freely supposed grievances and proposed remedies; and that the fitting remedy for evil counsels is good ones. Believing in the power of reason as applied through public discussion, they eschewed silence coerced by law—the argument of force in its worst form. Recognizing the occasional tyrannies of governing majorities, they amended the Constitution so that free speech and assembly should be guaranteed.

Fear of serious injury cannot alone justify suppressions of free speech and assembly. Men feared witches and burnt women. It is the function of speech to free men from the bondage of irrational fears. To justify suppression of free speech there must be reasonable ground to fear that serious evil will result if free speech is practiced. There must be reasonable ground to believe that the danger apprehended is imminent. There must be reasonable ground to believe that the evil to be prevented is a serious one. Every denunciation of existing law tends in some measure to increase the probability that there will be violation of it. Condonation of a breach enhances the probability. Expressions of approval add to the probability. Propagation of the criminal state of mind by teaching syndicalism increases it.

Advocacy of lawbreaking heightens it still further. But even advocacy of violation, however reprehensible morally, is not a justification for denying free speech where the advocacy falls short of incitement and there is nothing to indicate that the advocacy would be immediately acted on. The wide difference between advocacy and incitement, between preparation and attempt, between assembling and conspiracy, must be borne in mind. To support a finding of clear and present danger it must be shown either that immediate serious violence was to be expected or was advocated, or that the past conduct furnished reason to believe that such advocacy was then contemplated.

Those who won our independence by revolution were not cowards. They did not fear political change. They did not exalt order at the cost of liberty. To courageous, self-reliant men, with confidence in the power of free and fearless reasoning applied through the processes of popular government, no danger flowing from speech can be deemed clear and present, unless the incidence of the evil apprehended is so imminent that it may befall before there is opportunity for full discussion. If there be time to expose through discussion the falsehood and fallacies, to avert the evil by the processes of education, the remedy to be applied is more speech, not enforced silence. Only an emergency can justify repression. Such must be the rule if authority is to be reconciled with freedom. Such, in my opinion, is the command of the Constitution. . . .

Moreover, even imminent danger cannot justify resort to prohibition of these functions essential to effective democracy, unless the evil apprehended is relatively serious. Prohibition of free speech and assembly is a measure so stringent that it would be inappropriate as the means for averting a relatively trivial harm to society."

—*Whitney v. California* (1927). Justice Brandeis,
concurring, joined by Justice Holmes.

CHAPTER 35

When Senseless Violence Can Strengthen Free Expression Resolve (2025)

The true test of democratic values comes not during ordinary times, but when communities face their most challenging moments. In September 2025, the assassination of conservative activist Charlie Kirk at a campus event shocked the nation and could have deepened political divisions. Instead, something remarkable happened: student leaders across the political spectrum chose civil discourse over confrontation.

Bipartisan Student Leadership

Within hours of the tragedy, college Democrats and Republicans began issuing joint statements that demonstrated the practical application of free expression principles. The Rhode Island Young Republicans and Rhode Island Young Democrats were among the first, declaring: "We may disagree on policy, but we are united in our belief in the value of life, civil discourse, and mutual respect."

Ken Naylor, chairman of the Young Republicans, told ABC News that Kirk's death "hit home with a lot of activists" and that he immediately reached out to Democratic leaders to craft a unified response. "All of us believe that if you're independent, Republican, or Democrat, there's no reason for this to be happening. In this country, we have the right to express ourselves and nobody should be silenced," he said.[1]

This sentiment echoed across campuses nationwide. The Ohio College Republican Federation and College Democrats of Ohio rejected "political violence in all its forms," writing that "violence undermines the very foundations of our republic" and urging students to "foster a culture where disagreement never escalates to harm."[2]

Local Leadership in Action

At Ohio State University, student leaders warned that political violence "erodes trust in our institutions" and "threatens the very foundations of civil discourse." They reaffirmed their commitment to making OSU "a place where students feel safe to express their opinions, regardless of their political affiliation."

The Georgetown Bipartisan Coalition, Georgetown University College Democrats, and Georgetown University College Republicans emphasized that "the right to express one's political beliefs without fear for one's personal safety—particularly on college campuses—is fundamental to American life and a key component to a healthy, fully functioning democracy."

The Deeper Lesson

These student responses illustrate several crucial principles that every citizen can apply:

Local Action Over National Rhetoric: Rather than waiting for political leaders to set the tone, student leaders took immediate action in their own communities.

Shared Values Over Partisan Differences: They focused on democratic principles that transcend political party affiliation rather than relitigate policy disagreements.

Constructive Response to Crisis: Instead of using tragedy to score political points, they used it as an opportunity to strengthen democratic norms.

Youth Leading by Example: The next generation demonstrated that Americans can choose civil discourse even in the most polarizing circumstances.

This response validates a central theme of this book: Americans already possess the cultural capacity for democratic discourse. What's needed isn't government intervention or institutional reform, but citizens willing to model the behavior they want to see in their communities.

When faced with a moment that could have further divided an already polarized nation, young Americans chose to build bridges instead of walls. Their example shows that the practical application of First Amendment values isn't just possible—it's already happening when citizens decide to lead by example rather than wait for others to act.

CHAPTER 36

Honoring James Madison's First Amendment Legacy in Today's Polarized America (2025)

M*adison* is embedded in our daily lives. The epicenter of advertising is Madison Avenue in New York City. When we want to see the Knicks or the Rangers, and, more recently, Billy Joel play, where do we go? Madison Square Garden. The first modern luxury hotel in Washington, D.C., opened in 1963. President John F. Kennedy was there as the Madison Hotel welcomed its first guests.

That brings us to Dolley and James Madison, who are the namesakes for many of these institutions, and countless other sites and cities. Dolley Madison had been married previously—her name had been Dolley Todd—and she was seventeen years younger than James Madison. He ultimately went to an analog version of an online dating site at the time—Aaron Burr. It was Burr who introduced Dolley Todd to James Madison. And of course, Aaron Burr later turned out to be the person who murdered another of our nation's Founding Fathers, Alexander Hamilton.

Let's consider Dolley Madison first. We know that she loved to serve and eat ice cream with others. But part of this hospitality was because she was the first great social hostess in Washington, D.C. One of the great legacies that Dolley Madison left us (hopefully to be revived) is the spirit of bipartisanship. Once upon a time, we had an extremely partisan environment nationwide. In fact, Thomas Jefferson refused to meet with anyone who was not in his political party. There also was a lot of violence. Aaron Burr shot and killed Alexander Hamilton, as noted, and there were frequent duels and physical altercations over politics by other leading figures then.

Dolley Madison had a novel idea. "Can we bring all of these people together so we can begin to have a civil and constructive dialogue?" Hopefully, that expressed spirit can be revived at some point in time, given the obvious great rancor in our country now between our political parties and political tribes.

What is also interesting about Dolley Madison is that she was the first First Lady of the United States, as we understand the duties of that position today. Thomas Jefferson was the third president and was succeeded by James Madison. He had been widowed and did not have a partner. Thus, Dolley Madison, who was not married to him, essentially said, "I will volunteer to be your hostess when you have official events." She trained for her role.

So when Madison was elected, Dolley Madison officially became the first First Lady of the United States. Moreover, she is the only First Lady in the history of our country who was given an honorary seat on the floor of Congress, because she was such a powerful political figure. Put simply, Dolley Madison played a critical and important role in early American history.

James Madison was small in stature but very big in ideas. He was one of the seven Founding Fathers and had a critical role to play in the development of the US Constitution, and ultimately the Bill of Rights. Madison truly was a team player. In fact, he wrote: "The Constitution is not like the fabled Goddess of Wisdom, the offspring of a single brain. It ought to be regarded as the work of many hearts and hands."[1] Admirably, he wanted to share credit with his colleagues and peers.

Madison initially opposed the idea of the Bill of Rights, however. Ultimately, Thomas Jefferson persuaded him that citizens needed greater protection than the original Constitution offered. Madison responded, essentially saying, "I will pick up that mantle and I will develop these amendments to the Constitution." Those first ten amendments are what we call the Bill of Rights.

Perhaps just as critically, he wrote twenty-nine of the eighty-five essays that we know as *The Federalist Papers*—an incredible resource articulating the philosophy of how our Constitution and our Bill of

Rights were developed. In *Federalist Number 9*, which was one of the twenty-nine essays that Madison wrote, he said, "The people are the only legitimate fountain of power. And it is from that, that the constitutional charter, under which the several branches of government hold their power, is limited."

Madison was concerned about the potential overreach of government, which is reflected in the Bill of Rights. In essence, how do we build a wall between government and the people to prevent the government from going over that wall and encroaching on their personal liberties?

The forty-five words Madison wrote for the First Amendment were precise and elegant expressions of five essential freedoms. "Congress shall make no law respecting an establishment of religion, or prohibiting the free exercise thereof, or abridging the freedom of speech, or of the press, or the right of the people peaceably to assemble and to petition the government for a redress of grievances."

Unfortunately, James Madison would be dismayed if he were with us today. There now are sophisticated ways to measure how people perceive the First Amendment and its notions of free press and free speech. It's worthwhile to review the results of several recent national surveys for a flavor of how Americans envision the First Amendment in contemporary times.

According to a 2022 survey by the Knight Foundation, 89 percent of adults see freedom of speech as essential to democracy.[2] This is obviously good news; in comparison to some other data below, the contrast will be evident in their dramatic downward turn.

For example, a survey in July 2023 by the APM Research Lab found that only 45 percent of adults believe that democracy, while somewhat problematic, is the best system of government to have in place.[3] The Knight Foundation in 2022 found that only 59 percent felt that news organizations should not face government censorship when putting out the news. Sobering numbers, for sure, with more dire results continuing this year.[4]

Several major surveys have been released in 2024, principally by the Foundation for Individual Rights and Expression (FIRE), a leading national nonprofit organization that is involved in First Amendment advocacy and research.[5] FIRE found in its most recent survey that only

25 percent of Americans believe freedom of speech is secure. Sixty-nine percent believe it is off track and headed in the wrong direction.

The results from college campuses are just as sobering. Another FIRE survey, conducted in conjunction with the Cato Institute in early 2024, found that only 37 percent of students think it is never acceptable to shout down a speaker. Only 55 percent think it is never acceptable to block other students from hearing the speaker. And a growing number—27 percent in that survey—believe that violence can be an acceptable way to stop a campus speech.[6] These are all very alarming numbers.

An additional aspect of reliable survey research merits attention. It hits closer to home with respect to media and communications enterprises. In 2023, Gallup found that only 32 percent of Americans trust the news media and 39 percent have no confidence at all in the news media. The comparison with 2016 is quite dramatic. At that point in time, 27 percent had no confidence. Now, as noted, this number has risen to 39 percent.[7]

In terms of the current political climate assessed in this survey, although 58 percent of Democrats trust the news media, only 11 percent of Republicans and 29 percent of Independents do. Indeed, there is an extremely polarized environment with respect to trusting the news media. A survey by the respected Pew Research Center in 2023 found that 71 percent of respondents thought news and information was being made up and was a big problem for our country.[8]

Considering all this, it is timely to ask: "WWJMD—What Would James Madison Do?" Madison was not just a great constitutional architect; he also was a media mogul in his own time. Madison founded a newspaper called the *National Gazette*. He also founded the first political party, called the Democratic Republican Party. He then had the *National Gazette* essentially act as the media resource for the party. He used the *Gazette* to advance the ideology of the Democratic Republicans.

In some ways, the *National Gazette* was the Fox News or MSNBC of that era. Madison felt it was important and appropriate for media outlets to have sharp ideological distinctions. He was very proud of being able to start a publication, not with the idea of being fair and balanced, but with the idea that other publications would launch and have opposing views. He believed strongly in the idea of individual freedom—that all people should have the ability to hear information from many sources and to make decisions as a society. In 1791, when the Bill of Rights took effect, he wrote an essay called *Popular Basis of Political Authority*. "Public opinion sets bounds to every government," he observed, "and is the real sovereign in every free one."

It's not difficult to imagine what James Madison might say if he were with us now. He would recognize that media and communications companies, whether individually or through trade associations, are critical in both restoring confidence in our cherished First Amendment values and improving and enhancing trust in media. This is especially important this year, as Americans return to the ballot box to elect our forty-seventh president. Public opinion is essential, and media help drive public opinion.

According to FIRE, in 2023, only 40 percent of Americans could name one right protected by the First Amendment.[9] Freedom of speech is the right respondents named most often. But it should be noted that the number of those survey respondents who realized freedom of speech is protected under our Constitution only was 63 percent. Freedom of the press was named by a mere 20 percent. This gives a sense of why media and communications companies need to play a critical role in helping shape and improve public opinion around free speech and free press.

What might be done to heighten public awareness of the First Amendment? First, it would be beneficial if every media company and associated trade association put its forty-five words on its website, or had a pop-up there, and put them on their social media platforms, too.

Many Americans have never seen what the First Amendment actually looks like. We all know how to recite the Pledge of Allegiance, but most of us don't know how to recite the First Amendment. Visualizing it again and again can help everyone see how powerful those words can be when they're put together.

It would also be useful if media companies and trade associations went to the public libraries in their local communities and said, "We will make an attractive banner with the words of the First Amendment that will be hung at the entrance for patrons to see as they walk into the library."

Libraries would be happy to accept this gift and proud to display it. After all, the First Amendment covers the right to read everything that is in a library. Additionally, media companies and associated trade associations could donate a collection of books about free speech and free press to individual local libraries. When children and other patrons came in, they would see a prominent display of First Amendment books on a dedicated bookshelf. Of course, we are now in the era of ebooks, which could be made available digitally to a wide audience that may access library resources remotely rather than in person.

Those with longer memories may remember that in 1976, CBS pioneered something called the *Bicentennial Minute* to commemorate our country's two hundredth anniversary. It committed a minute of valuable airtime throughout the year so that a celebrity or someone in news or sports could speak briefly about our Constitution and our country's history.

What if once again there was a new effort to produce the equivalent of those CBS Bicentennial Minutes? Beginning in 2026 to coincide with America 250, there could be a new one-minute video that's posted, produced, or perhaps sponsored by a rotating group of media companies and organizations every day—in mass media and on social media platforms alike. Again, this initiative could help raise public opinion and help reverse the downward First Amendment course that the surveys are showing with alarming consistency.

Perhaps most importantly, in media organizations today, there are new generations being hired, along with intergenerational groups of people working together. Alas, it would be too much to assume that there is a high level of knowledge of, or appreciation for, the First Amendment among them.

Internally, media companies and associated trade associations need to do more in terms of education and discussion around the First Amendment. Their employees are the shapers of public opinion, which makes staff education exceedingly important. No field has benefited more from the First Amendment than the media. It is in the business interest of media companies and trade associations—as well as a real civic responsibility as stewards of free speech and free press—for them to visibly support the First Amendment strongly in multiple ways.

Despite the gloomy statistics, there clearly still is room for optimism. If we devote proper attention and focus in this area, we all can play a part in keeping alive the profound lessons about the power of the First Amendment and its enduring values that James Madison left behind.

Afterword

As we look toward America's semiquincentennial and beyond, we must ask ourselves whether this is the country we want to be—one where people are afraid to speak their minds, where disagreement is treated as heresy, and where the marketplace of ideas has been replaced by ideological monopolies? And if not, what will be our collective course forward?

> "We are celebrating 250 years of the founding of this great nation, that founding document, the Declaration of Independence that this great experiment on which we embarked together 250 years ago, that we are endowed by our creator with certain unalienable rights. . . . We desperately need our country. We desperately need leaders in our country, but more than the leaders, we just need every single person in this country to think about where we are and where we want to be—to ask ourselves, *Is this it?*"
> —Governor Spencer Cox (R-UT)

> "We the people must never accept government threats to our freedom of speech. Efforts by leaders to pressure artists, journalists, and companies with retaliation for their speech strike at the heart of what it means to live in a free country."
> —Meryl Streep and Tom Hanks, open letter organized by the American Civil Liberties Union (ACLU), September 2025

"Time to defend our values—the values that have made this country the freest, most tolerant society in the history of the world—without hesitation or apology."

                   —Bari Weiss, founder, *The Free Press*

Acknowledgments

I am grateful to so many people who have influenced my own First Amendment journey, instilling in me a continued passion for free speech and free press values. Their insights have been invaluable.

Great appreciation to Greg Lukianoff for his superb contribution to this book and his impactful work as a stalwart free expression champion.

Kudos, too, to other national treasures promoting free speech and press—Floyd Abrams, Nadine Strossen, and Geoffrey Stone.

Chief Judge David L. Bazelon represented broad and deep jurisprudential thinking about the First Amendment. The constitutional conversations I had with him early in my career have had a profound impact on me.

During my formative educational years—from high school through law school—I had the benefit of an extraordinary group of teachers, professors, and academic advisors: Arza Dean, Elaine Levine, Frederick Crouter, Alexander Bell, William Clifford, Frances Lazarus, Judith Paul, Austin B. Johnson III, Franklyn S. Haiman, John L. McKnight, Irving J. Rein, Lawrence W. Lichty, Don R. LeDuc, Charles Sherman, Joanne Cantor, Ordean Ness, Edwin Black, Stephen Barnett, Paul Mishkin, Jesse Choper, and Herma Hill Kay.

Numerous lawyers have been important to me, as well. These include my cherished mentors Henry Geller, Newton N. Minow, Morton I. Hamburg, Geoffrey Cowan, Monroe E. Price, Paul Weiler, Richard E. Wiley, and Bertram Fields.

Other legal stalwarts of note include Judge Douglas Ginsburg, Daniel L. Brenner, Harry Plotkin, George Shapiro, Mark Goldberg, Howard Nemerovski, David Cantor, Bruce Sunstein, Rikki Klieman, Christopher Fager, Stuart Shorenstein, Tedson Meyers, Charlie Firestone, Michael Fricklas, Ronald Cass, Robert D. Joffe, Maxwell M. Blecher, Bonnie Eskenazi, Bruce Goodman, Christopher Wolf, Howard Liberman, Ann

Bobeck, Patrick Campbell, Phillip Spector, Kevin Smith, Gene Korf, Sally Stevens, Fabio Bertoni, Robert Sachs, Carole E. Handler, Anthony Romero, Burt Neuborne, David Cole, Lucy Dalglish, Bob Corn-Revere, Robert McDowell, Michele Farquhar, Jules Polonetsky, Randy Tritell, Blair Levin, Howard Homonoff, Michael Whelan, Ronald K.L. Collins, Randolph May, Jack Balkin, Tracie Brown, Kevin Michels, Jeffrey Pollock, Kenneth Marcus, Eleanor Barrett, Clare Norins, Emily Keimig, Jerry Papazian, Michael Sanders, Dick Tofel, Brad Morgan, Theodore Boutrous Jr., Adonis Hoffman, Lonnie Brown, Beth Ford, Alan Blaustein, Jane Kirtley, Shaun Clark, Jerry Fritz, Danielle Coffey, Kathleen Kirby, Abraham Sofaer, Ken Hagen, Ike Williams, Charles B. Ortner, Larry Irving, Glenn Reynolds, Tamara Sepper, Erwin G. Krasnow, Cameron Kerry, Patricia Diaz Dennis, David Apatoff, Erwin Chemerinsky, and Ken Basin. All have offered sage perspectives, advice, and counsel along the way.

Within academia, I have been blessed with many wonderful colleagues: Albert Pickerell, Fred Cate, Marty Linsky, Robert Frieden, Peter Blanck, Harvey Jassem, Barry Umansky, Ron Kovac, Anne Klinefelter, Everette E. Dennis, Ellen Hume, Miriam Berg, John Dale, Norman Marcus, Jay Gillette, David Klatell, Wenhong Chen, Maria Lombard, Thomas Mascaro, Anupam Chander, Nikhil Moro, Barb Kaye, Patrick Burkart, Bob Pepper, Craig LaMay, Margaret Hu, Dom Caristi, Jonathan Peters, Patricia Phalen, Martha Minow, David Kennedy, Ron Rizzuto, John Carey, Rob Wicks, C. Raj Kumar, Arpan Banerjee, Adam Mossoff, Rona Kaufman, Greg Pitts, Ken Paulson, John Palfrey, Elena Kagan, Denis Simon, Sanford Ungar, Nicholas Lemann, Lawrence Summers, Wat Hopkins, Rick Jewell, Terry Fisher, Nana Sarian, Mark Wu, Jeannie Suk Gersen, Phil Napoli, Allison Stanger, Thane Rosenbaum, Peter Gross, Douglas Blaze, Joan MacLeod Heminway, Marianne Wanamaker, Josh Dunn, and Robert B. McKay.

Professional colleagues representing various disciplines have enriched me in many ways, too. They include Bill Arthur, Ned Schnurman, Jane Harman, Fred Friendly, Margaret Sullivan, Bob Katz, Meg King, Bob Stearns, Walter S. Baer, Ruth Vitale, Bruce DuMont, George de Lama, Susan Kohler Reed, Joyce Tudryn, Edward Felsenthal, Roslyn Layton, Deb Gordon, Christie Hefner, Amanda Warren, Tom Kemp, Michael Graham, Benjamin Slivka, Karen Tumulty, Kyle

Pope, Katie Hannah, Tara Palmieri, Mike Allen, Sara Fischer, Marc Ransford, Ryan McKenna, James Risen, Ren LaForme, Patrick Butler, Mark Miller, David Suissa, Rufus Friday, John Milewski, Nico Perrino, Heather Birks, Daniel Lelchuk, Christopher Finan, Susanna Coto, Eric Cervone, Joyce Kulhawik, Andrew Davidson, Robin Rennison, Deanna Davis, Drew Griffiths, Megan Casey, Margaret Hogan, Carey Cranston, Robin Blinder, Mike Blinder, Joan Hamburg, Suzie Katz, Richard Kaplar, Margery Kraus, Vivian Schiller, Ann Margolin, Barry Glassner, Jack Moline, Renée Edelman, Robin Blatt, Dan Glickman, Brent Crane, Jonathan Adelstein, Sandra Baer, Adrian Basora, Jeff Frazier, Joan Myers, John Della Volpe, Cecile Willems, Gabriela Oliván, Scott Wallsten, Sarah Oh Lam, and Richard Carlson.

My teaching has enabled me to work with an extraordinary group of students around the world. I am immensely proud of Matt Bruck, Mark Seidenfeld, Sandra Bresnick, Marc Kenny, Eric German, Shawn Ambwani, Jeffrey Carlisle, Olaf Groth, Brett Perlman, R.D. Sahl, Jennifer Paul, Ariel Shpiegel, J. Hillyer Jennings, Ruchi Desai, Richard Lehun, Mark Mower, Beverly Banks, and Kathryn Kavanaugh, along with thousands of others I have taught, from forty-eight countries on five continents, in undergraduate, graduate, professional, and executive education programs.

Cherished friends from kindergarten onward continue. Thanks to Andy Cohen, Bob Males, Rick Schultz, Cornell Christianson, and Nell Minow.

Special appreciation to my superb literary agent, Karen Gantz, for her continuing support and wise counsel.

The Skyhorse Publishing team has been extraordinary on all fronts, among them Tony Lyons, Michael Campbell, Rachel Marble, Janina Krayer, Kate Hatcher, and David Ter-Avanesyan.

Thomas Gensemer is a welcome addition to our family and invaluable both personally and professionally.

Gloria Z. Greenfield and our children—Daniel, Rachel, and Gabriel—are always valued for their deeply held and freely expressed viewpoints. Through them, I have learned that the First Amendment and its values can serve both our closest relationships and America's larger national aspirations that endure, as we celebrate our nation's 250th anniversary and beyond.

About the Author

Stuart N. Brotman is America's leading public scholar on free expression. Brotman's public scholarship takes complex free expression ideas out of academic ivory towers and makes them accessible in kitchen table conversations, coffee shop debates, and civic discussions that shape communities.

He is Digital Media Laureate and a Distinguished Senior Fellow at The Media Institute, where he also serves on its First Amendment Council.

Brotman served in four Presidential administrations on a bipartisan basis. He was the first Visiting Professor of Entertainment and Media Law at Harvard Law School and held concurrent appointments in digital media at Harvard's Berkman Klein Center for Internet & Society and MIT's Program in Comparative Media Studies.

As an interdisciplinary tenured Professor of Journalism and Media at the University of Tennessee, Knoxville, he served as the inaugural Alvin and Sally Beaman Professor of Journalism and Media Law, Enterprise, and Leadership, and as the inaugural Howard Distinguished Endowed Professor of Media Management and Law.

He was also the Fulbright-Nokia Distinguished Chair in Information and Communications Technologies at the University of Helsinki.

Brotman is an elected member of The American Law Institute. His career spans legal scholarship and practice, media and technology policy, journalism, and civic education. He has participated in several First Amendment Supreme Court cases and has provided expert counsel on free expression issues to government agencies; media, entertainment, technology companies; and news organizations.

He is a frequent contributor to prominent publications, including the *New York Times*, the *Washington Post*, *Los Angeles Times*, *Forbes*,

The Hill, USA Today Network, Bloomberg Businessweek, and *Editor & Publisher.* His essays also make him internationally visible as a global expert on free expression through massive online platforms such as Yahoo! News, MSN, and AOL.

Brotman has appeared as a sought-after commentator for C-SPAN, CNN, ABC News, NBC News, NPR, Reuters TV, the Canadian Broadcasting Corporation, and on numerous podcasts, offering timely constitutional and cultural analyses on topical free expression issues worldwide. He is also a regularly featured speaker at major conferences on five continents.

His perspective is shaped by decades-long experience teaching college and professional school students from forty-eight countries in six separate academic disciplines—law, business, public policy, international affairs, media, and journalism—a unique vantage point that brings a genuinely global and multidisciplinary approach to current and future questions of speech and press freedom.

Brotman remains active as an influential thought leader in law, policy, and academic networks dedicated to strengthening democratic culture in the US and globally. Through his unparalleled combination of legal expertise, media authority, and cross-cultural academic experience, he is an indispensable voice articulating the free expression challenges and opportunities facing American democracy now and in the years ahead.

Endnotes

CHAPTER 1

1   Freedom Forum, "Where America Stands: Report 2025," Washington, DC: Freedom Forum, 2025. https://www.freedomforum.org/wp-content/uploads/2025/09/Freedom-Forum-Where-America-Stands-Report-2025-2.pdf.

CHAPTER 2

1   Pope Francis, "Annual Address to Diplomats," Vatican, January 10, 2022. https://www.catholicnewsagency.com/news/250062/pope-francis-laments-cancel-culture-in-annual-address-to-diplomats.

CHAPTER 3

1   Barry Popik, "Make a Federal Case (Out of It)," BarryPopik.com, https://www.barrypopik.com/index.php/new_york_city/entry/make_a_federal_case_out_of_it.

2   Bernard M. Baruch, "Every man has a right to his opinion, but no man has a right to be wrong in his facts." *Deming Headlight*, January 6, 1950, as cited in LibQuotes, https://libquotes.com/bernard-baruch/quote/lbg6n1u.

3   Pew Research Center, "Free Speech & Press—Research and Data," Pew Research Center, 2018. https://www.pewresearch.org/topic/politics-policy/political-issues/free-speech-press/.

CHAPTER 4

1   The Kalven Committee, Report on the University's Role in Political and Social Action, University of Chicago, 1967. https://provost.uchicago.edu/sites/default/files/documents/reports/KalvenReport.pdf.

2   Geoffrey R. Stone, et al., Report of the Committee on Freedom of Expression, University of Chicago, 2018. https://provost.uchicago.edu/sites/default/files/documents/reports/FOECommitteeReport.pdf.

CHAPTER 5

1   Foundation for Individual Rights and Expression and College Pulse, "2026 College Free Speech Rankings," FIRE, 2025. https://rankings.thefire.org/.

2   Poorvu Center for Teaching and Learning, Yale University, "Writing Center Handouts," 2025. https://poorvucenter.yale.edu/writing-center-handouts.

CHAPTER 6

1   *Counterman v. Colorado*, 600 U.S. 66 (2023). https://www.law.cornell.edu/supremecourt/text/22-138.

CHAPTER 7

1   Jenny S. Martinez, "Next Steps on Protests and Free Speech," Stanford Law School, March 22, 2023. https://law.stanford.edu/wp-content/uploads/2023/03/Next-Steps-on-Protests-and-Free-Speech.pdf.
2   Stanford Law School, "Letter of Apology to Judge Duncan," March 11, 2023. https://law.stanford.edu/documents/letter-of-apology-to-judge-duncan.
3   Gallup, "Confidence in U.S. Supreme Court Sinks to Historic Low," June 22, 2022. https://news.gallup.com/poll/394103/confidence-supreme-court-sinks-historic-low.aspx.
4   David Lat, "Dean Jenny Martinez Speaks Out About The Protest of Judge Duncan," Original Jurisdiction, March 23, 2023. https://davidlat.substack.com/p/dean-jenny-martinez-speaks-out-about.

CHAPTER 8

1   Heterodox Academy, "Campus Expression Survey," Heterodox Academy, 2024. https://heterodoxacademy.org/campus-expression-survey/.
2   Nicole Barbaro et al., "The Universal Problem of Campus Expression," Heterodox Academy, September 2024, https://content.heterodoxacademy.org/uploads/HxA_CES_UniversalProblem_FINAL.pdf.
3   Foundation for Individual Rights and Expression (FIRE), "Silence in the Classroom: The 2024 FIRE Faculty Survey Report," November 12, 2024. https://www.thefire.org/facultyreport.
4   Samuel Abrams, "Self-Censorship on College Campuses Is Widespread and Getting Worse," American Enterprise Institute, March 6, 2023.

CHAPTER 9

1   Central Texas College, "Campus Zero Tolerance Policy," 2024. https://www.ctcd.edu/locations/central-campus/campus-safety-wellness/safety-and-security/campus-police1/campus-rules-regulations-and-policies/campus-zero-tolerance-policy/.

CHAPTER 10

1   *Reno vs. ACLU*. 521 U.S. 844 (1997). https://supreme.justia.com/cases/federal/us/521/844/
2   Supreme Court of the United States, *Packingham v. North Carolina*, 582 U.S. 98 (2017). https://www.supremecourt.gov/opinions/16pdf/15-1194_08l1.pdf.

CHAPTER 11

1   Judge Mark E. Walker, order granting preliminary injunction, *Pernell et al. v. Florida Board of Governors*, U.S. District Court, Northern District of Florida, Nov. 17, 2022, p. 8, https://www.chronicle.com/article/conjuring-orwell-florida -judge-blasts-dystopian-ban-on-woke-instruction.

CHAPTER 12

1   Jack Goldsmith, as cited in Jack Goldsmith's faculty profile, Harvard Law School. https://hls.harvard.edu/faculty/jack-l-goldsmith/.

CHAPTER 13

1   *Miller v. College of Policing*, EWHC 225 (Admin) (UK, 2020), para 250: https://www.judiciary.uk/wp-content/uploads/2020/02/miller-v-college-of -police-judgment.pdf.

CHAPTER 14

1   Fox Business. "Big Tech running over FTC, agency needs revamp: Sen. Josh Hawley," February 10, 2020. https://www.foxbusiness.com/technology/big-tech -josh-hawley-ftc.
2   *Red Lion Broadcasting Co. v. Federal Communications Commission*, 395 U.S. 367 (1969). https://supreme.justia.com/cases/federal/us/395/367/.

CHAPTER 15

1   Freedom Forum, "2022 Update—Where America Stands," March 2022, https: //www.freedomforum.org/where-america-stands/2022-update/.

CHAPTER 18

1   Federal Communications Commission, "In re Citizen's Complaint Against Pacifica Foundation Station WBAI (FM), 56 F.C.C.2d 94 (1975)," as cited in *Hofstra Law Review*, https://scholarlycommons.law.hofstra.edu/cgi/viewcontent .cgi?article=1250&context=hlr.

CHAPTER 19

1   Stuart N. Brotman, "An Insider Glimpse into the Story of the Pentagon Papers Case," *Nieman Reports*, March 3, 2025, https://niemanreports.org/new-york -times-pentagon-papers-book/.

CHAPTER 21

1   *CBS v. Democratic Nat'l Committee*, 412 U.S. 94 (1973). https://supreme.justia .com/cases/federal/us/412/94/

CHAPTER 22

1   Tom Wheeler, "An 'Aha' Moment: Understanding the Public Interest," *Variety*, January 19, 2017. https://variety.com/2017/biz/news/tom-wheeler-fcc-farewell -1201964219/.

2   Federal Communications Commission, "Public Interest Obligations of Television Broadcast Licensees," 65 Fed. Reg. 3623 (Jan. 26, 2000), https://www.federalregister.gov/documents/2000/01/26/00-1794/public-interest-obligations-of-television-broadcast-licensees.

3   Newton N. Minow, "Television and the Public Interest," speech, National Association of Broadcasters, May 9, 1961, as reprinted in the *Federal Communications Law Journal* 55, no. 3 (2003): 397. https://www.americanrhetoric.com/speeches/newtonminow.htm.

4   Ibid.

5   Ibid.

6   Stuart N. Brotman, "Revisiting the Broadcast Public Interest Standard in Communications Law and Regulation," Brookings, March 8, 2022, https://www.brookings.edu/articles/revisiting-the-broadcast-public-interest-standard-in-communications-law-and-regulation/

7   Ibid.

8   Ibid.

9   Henry Geller, quoted in "Broadcasting and the Public Trustee Notion: A Failed Promise," *Harvard Journal of Law & Public Policy* 10 (Winter 1987): 87, https://www.worldradiohistory.com/BOOKSHELF-ARH/Commentary/Abandoned-in-the_Wasteland-Minow.pdf.

10 Peter W. Huber, "Congress cannot exercise effective oversight," *Law and Disorder in Cyberspace: Abolish the FCC and Let Common Law Rule the Telecosm*, Oxford University Press, 1997, p. 57.

11 Randolph J. May, "The Public Interest Standard: Is It Too Indeterminate to Be Constitutional?" *Federal Communications Law Journal* 53, no. 1 (2000): 43. (p. 124).

CHAPTER 23

1   Brendan Carr, X (formerly Twitter), November 17, 2024, https://x.com/BrendanCarrFCC/status/1858327922810970327?lang=en.

2   Ibid.

3   Federal Communications Commission, as quoted in Stuart N. Brotman, "Revisiting the broadcast public interest standard in communications law and regulation," Brookings, March 8, 2022. https://www.brookings.edu/articles/revisiting-the-broadcast-public-interest-standard-in-communications-law-and-regulation/.

4   Brendan Carr, as quoted in Reuters, "Trump's FCC Chair Carr uses old powers in new ways to rein in media companies," September 19, 2025, https://www.reuters.com/business/media-telecom/trumps-fcc-chair-carr-uses-old-powers-new-ways-rein-media-companies-2025-09-19/.

CHAPTER 24

1   NBC News, February 23, 2017, https://www.nbcnews.com/politics/white-house/trump-launches-attack-unnamed-press-sources-n725226.

2   *CBS v. Democratic National Committee*, 412 U.S. 94 (1973).

CHAPTER 26

1   John S. and James L. Knight Foundation, "Future of the First Amendment 2022: High Schooler Views on Speech Over Time," May 24, 2022, https://knightfoundation.org/reports/future-of-the-first-amendment-2022-high-schooler-views-on-speech-over-time/.

CHAPTER 27

1   Jenny Gross, "How Finland is Teaching a Generation to Spot Misinformation," *New York Times.* January 10, 2023. https://www.nytimes.com/2023/01/10/world/europe/finland-misinformation-classes.html.

CHAPTER 29

1   Adam Liptak, "In Supreme Court Opinions, Web Links to Nowhere," *New York Times*, September 23, 2013, https://www.nytimes.com/2013/09/24/us/politics/in-supreme-court-opinions-clicks-that-lead-nowhere.html. (Summarizes analysis by Professor Allison Orr Larsen.)

CHAPTER 30

1   "A Free and Responsive Press," a report by the Twentieth Century Fund Task Force for a National News Council (New York: Twentieth Century Fund, 1973).

2   Patrick Brogan, *Spiked: The Short Life and Death of the National News Council*, Transaction Publishers, 1973. [Quote attributed to Bill Arthur within the volume.]

3   Gallup, "Trust in Media at New Low of 28% in U.S.," October 2, 2025, https://news.gallup.com/poll/695762/trust-media-new-low.aspx.

4   Pew Research Center, "Media Mistrust Has Been Growing for Decades—Does It Matter?" October 16, 2024, https://www.pew.org/en/trend/archive/fall-2024/media-mistrust-has-been-growing-for-decades-does-it-matter.

5   Jonathan M. Ladd, "Why Americans Hate the Media and How It Matters," Princeton University Press, 2012.

6   Jesse Holcomb, Pew Research Center, as cited in "Media Mistrust Has Been Growing for Decades—Does It Matter?" October 16, 2024, https://www.pew.org/en/trend/archive/fall-2024/media-mistrust-has-been-growing-for-decades-does-it-matter.

7   Ralph Otwell, quoted in "Twilight of Press Freedom: The Rise of People's Journalism" (LEA's Communication Series), 2004, p. xxi, http://ndl.ethernet.edu.et/bitstream/123456789/16006/1/53.pdf.pdf.

8   Pew Research Center, "Americans See Skepticism of News Media as Healthy, Say Public Trust in the Institution Can Improve," August 31, 2020. https://www.pewresearch.org/journalism/2020/08/31/americans-see-skepticism-of-news-media-as-healthy-say-public-trust-in-the-institution-can-improve/.

9   Patrick Brogan, *Spiked: The Short Life and Death of the National News Council* (New York: Greenwood Press, 1985).

10 Ibid.

CHAPTER 31

1   Ithielde de Sola Pool, *Technologies of Freedom*, Cambridge, MA: Belknap Press, 1983. https://books.google.com/books/about/Technologies_of_Freedom.html ?id=BzLXGUxV4CkC.
2   Ibid.
3   Ibid.

CHAPTER 32

1   Freedom House, "Freedom in the World 2027: The Annual Survey of Political Rights and Civil Liberties," Freedom House, 2027. https://freedomhouse.org /report/freedom-world.

CHAPTER 33

1   Tim Davie, as cited in BBC News, October 29, 2020. https://pressgazette.co .uk/news/bbc-social-media-guidelines-ban-virtue-signalling-criticism-of-colleagues -and-breaking-stories-on-your-own-accounts.

CHAPTER 35

1   ABC News, "College Democrats and Republicans send unified messages after Kirk's death," September 13, 2025. https://abcnews.go.com/Politics/college -democrats-republicans-send-unified-messages-after-kirks/story?id=125557254.
2   Ibid.

CHAPTER 36

1   James Madison, letter to William Cogswell, March 10, 1834, Founders Online, National Archives, https://founders.archives.gov/documents/Madison/99-02 -02-2952.
2   Knight Foundation & Ipsos, "Future of the First Amendment 2022: High Schooler Views on Speech Over Time," Knight Foundation, May 24, 2022, https://knight foundation.org/reports/future-of-the-first-amendment-2022-high-schooler -views-on-speech-over-time/.
3   APM Research Lab, "Public Perceptions of Freedom of Expression on University Campuses," AP-NORC/University of Chicago, July 2023, https://apnorc .org/wp-content/uploads/2023/09/APNORC-UChicago-Freedom-of-Speech -Report-Final.pdf.
4   Knight Foundation & Ipsos, "Future of the First Amendment 2022: High Schooler Views on Speech Over Time," Knight Foundation, May 24, 2022, https://knightfoundation.org/reports/future-of-the-first-amendment-2022 -high-schooler-views-on-speech-over-time/.
5   Foundation for Individual Rights and Expression (FIRE), "2024 College Free Speech Rankings," 2024, https://www.thefire.org/research-learn/2024-college -free-speech-rankings.

6   Foundation for Individual Rights and Expression (FIRE) & Cato Institute, "FIRE/Cato Institute Student Freedom of Speech Survey, 2024," https://www.thefire.org/research-learn/2024-college-free-speech-rankings.

7   Gallup, "Trust in Media at New Low of 28% in U.S," October 2, 2025, https://news.gallup.com/poll/695762/trust-media-new-low.aspx.

8   Pew Research Center, "Striking findings from 2023," December 8, 2023. https://www.pewresearch.org/short-reads/2023/12/08/striking-findings-from-2023/.

9   Foundation for Individual Rights and Expression (FIRE), "Can You Name the Five First Amendment Rights?" Survey, 2024. https://www.thefire.org/resources/first-amendment-center/can-you-name-the-five-first-amendment-rights-2024-survey.